The Inter-Fa...
The New Age E...

THE INTER-FAITH MOVEMENT

The New Age Enters the Church

Herbert J. Pollitt
M.A., M.Litt., Ph.D.

THE BANNER OF TRUTH TRUST

THE BANNER OF TRUTH TRUST
3 Murrayfield Road, Edinburgh EH 12 6EL
P.O. Box 621, Carlisle, Pennsylvania 17013, U.S.A.

★

© *Herbert J. Pollitt 1996*
First Published 1996
ISBN 0 85151 680 7

★

Typset in 10½/12pt Linotron Plantin
at The Spartan Press Limited,
Lymington, Hants
Printed and bound in Finland by WSOY

IN GRATEFUL MEMORY OF MY
FATHER, CHARLES POLLITT,
PREACHER OF THE WRITTEN WORD OF GOD,
AND MY MOTHER, KATE POLLITT,
LOVER OF THE WORD INCARNATE.

Contents

Contents

CHAPTER V   INTER-FAITH AND THE NEW AGE

Preface

For this study I am indebted to Lambeth Palace for supplying me with a copy of Dr Runcie's Francis Younghusband Memorial Lecture, to Miss Cicely Blackdown, secretary of Bishop Henderson in the Roman Catholic Archdiocese of Southwark, who provided me with the material from the papal organ *L'Osservatore Romano*, and to the Rev T. Higton for permission to use his critique of the Church of England's guidelines on multi-faith worship. This is available from him at Emmanuel Church Office, Main Road, Hawkwell, Hockley, Essex, and is mostly serious study. Lastly, I should like to thank my publishers for their encouragement and their efficiency in dealing with an intractable typescript.

Nothing is implied about the eternal status of any one discussed. It is their theologies and practices which are called into question. One can only repeat with James, 'These things ought not so to be' (3:1). What I have written goes out with the prayer that it might reach many who are participating, even marginally, in inter-faith activity, to make them aware of the extent to which they are being blown about by the spirit of the age instead of furthering the kingdom of God.

H. J. Pollitt
10 April 1995

CHAPTER I

The Inter-Faith Movement:
A Preliminary Survey

1: *The Inter-Faith Movement: A Preliminary Survey*

On 26 September, 1902 a new window in the south transept of Westminster Abbey was dedicated. Surrounding Christ in the centre, the inner circle contains sixteen figures symbolical of the virtues and the orders of angels. The outer circle is filled by thirty-two figures chosen to represent the preparation of the world for his coming. In the upper half are the sixteen Jewish prophets; in the lower half, Enoch, Abraham, Moses, David, Solomon, Job, Ezra and Sirach, also from the chosen people of Israel, and from the Gentile world Plato, Aristotle, Aeschylus, the Sybil, Zoroaster, one of the magi, Virgil and Seneca. Christ, then is central, and biblical characters preponderate, while the classical world takes precedence over the Eastern religions. The window is an expression of the current philosophical idealism; the Eastern religions have only a marginal place. But trends were already at work which were ultimately to reverse the position to remove Christ to the periphery and bring Eastern religions to the fore. The purpose of this study is to demonstrate the marginalization of Christ in the emerging global religious, cultural and political consciousness of the age.

In 1879, the Orientalist Sir Edwin Arnold did much to familiarize the English public with the teachings of Buddhism by his epic poem on the legends and life of the Buddha, 'The Light of Asia'. His 'Light of the World' (1891) brought Hinduism into general notice although it did not gain such a wide circulation. Of greater importance was his translation of the *Bhagavad-Gita*, the epitome of Hinduism, which was to awaken in no less a figure than Gandhi a deeper appreciation of his own religious tradition.

The interest in Eastern and non-Christian religions was by no means confined to England at this time. In 1893, the World's

3

Columbian Exhibition, a world fair for the celebration of man's technological achievement, was held in Chicago. In conjunction with it a World Parliament of Religions was held to show the contribution of religion to humanity. Over a period of seventeen days this brought together delegates representing not only the major branches of Christianity, Catholic, Orthodox and Protestant, but also Theism, Judaism, Islam, Hinduism, Buddhism, Jainism, Taoism, Confucianism and Zoroastrianism. The contemporary Archbishop of Canterbury, Edward White Benson, refused to attend on the grounds that participation would compromise the uniqueness of Christianity and imply that other religions were its equals. E. J. Eitel, a missionary in Hong Kong, issued a forthright condemnation, accusing the organizers of 'unconsciously planning treason against Christ' and of 'playing fast and loose . . . with false religions'.[1] This inter-faith gathering set in motion an impetus which has gathered and has continued to gather increasing momentum ever since.

Although its originators and their successors were not inactive in the meantime, one of the most significant advances of the inter-faith movement was the foundation in 1936 of the World Congress of Faiths by Sir Francis Younghusband, soldier, explorer, diplomat, and mystic, who had fallen deeply under the spell of Oriental religions during lengthy sojourns in Tibet and India. On a mountain facing Lhasa he had said in 1904, 'I had visions of a far greater religion yet to be, and of a god as much greater than our English God as a Himalayan giant is greater than an English hill'.[2] In 1924 he was invited to give the opening address at a religious conference at the British Empire Exhibition, where Hindus, Muslims, Buddhists and animists also spoke. In 1934 he was sponsored on a lecture tour of America by the World Fellowship of Faiths founded ten years previously by a Hindu and a Communist. This body held its first world congress at the Chicago World Fair in 1933 under the direction of ex-President Hoover and Jane Addams, a former associate of Lenin. It subsequently held a series of parliaments of faiths in various countries, which concluded with a gathering in New York in 1949, where an unprecedented inter-faith service was held in which fifteen priests and ministers of the most diverse religions participated.

4

The Inter-Faith Movement: A Preliminary Survey

In 1951 the World Congress of Faiths stated its aim in a brochure entitled *The World Congress of Faiths – Its Objects, Message and Work*:

The object of the World Congress of Faiths is to promote the spirit of fellowship among mankind and to do so through religion – through religion, however, interpreted in its universal and widest sense – a sense far transcending its particular expression in any one of the world's faiths, and penetrating to that divine essence we believe to be common to all . . . In our search for eternal truth, we enquire what the various religions offer to help us. Freed from all sense of intolerance, arrogance or condescension, we endeavour while maintaining our own faiths to learn what the worshippers of Brahma and Jehovah and Allah, what the followers of Zoroaster, Laotze, Confucius, Buddha and of Jesus were and are. The World Fellowship of Faiths is the building of a fellowship . . . which will guide mankind towards truth, the Kingdom of righteousness and brotherhood and peace.

In pursuit of this aim it announced its intention to bring pressure to bear upon national governments. Political leaders have been increasingly involved in the inter-faith movement from its inception. A participant in the inaugural meeting of the World Congress, and subsequently its Vice-President and Patron, was Dr S. Radhakrishnan, whose career embraced the direction of the United National Educational, Scientific and Cultural Organization, and the presidency and vice-presidency of India.

The religious faith of Younghusband has been examined by his biographer George Seaver. He tells us that Younghusband nourished his mind during his sojourn in the Gobi desert on the works of Darwin, which came to him as a revelation. His view of Christ was shaped by Renan's *Life of Jesus*, Seeley's *Ecce Homo* and Tolstoy's *The Kingdom of God is Within You*. It follows that it was the human not the divine Christ who attracted him. He rejected the doctrine of original sin on the ground that creation was a process of growth from low beginnings to a higher condition of life, thus illegitimately transforming the theory of evolution from a belief about physical origins into a theological dogma. He repudiated the unique divinity of Christ as involving a difference in kind between him and us. As he saw it, the doctrine of justification by faith and the supernatural elements of

Christianity were incrustations upon the simplicity of essential Christian faith. The divine spirit, a living flame in Christ, was latent in all men because they were all children of the same Father. This Father was not to be approached through petitionary prayer; prayer was rather in Seaver's words, 'the up-welling of His Spirit within us, deep calling to deep'.[3] He abhorred the idea of God as providence: again in Seaver's summary, 'not passive dependence upon him for our material needs but active co-operation with him in His divine purposes – this was our high purpose and our serious responsibility'.[4] But Younghusband can speak for himself. Seaver quotes a passage from a book he wrote in 1923, *The Gleam*. Describing his beliefs in the third person, Younghusband maintained:

The appearance of Christ on earth he regarded as the most important fact of human history. No other event had had anything like so great an influence on the course of the world . . . But Christ was plainly a development along the line of the holy men of God. If he were to be called divine then some few other men would have to be called divine. He had reached a higher level of being than ordinary men had attained. And he had manifested a higher quality. But in this he was rather the forerunner to show the way to other men, than of a different order of being. And other men might in the course of time reach that level and display that quality. He could not be considered a *complete* manifestation of God, a *complete* expression of God's will and intention, a complete full and final relevation of God.[5]

Here is no endeavour to uphold the Christian faith in the spirit of the stated aim of the World Congress of Faiths, but an expression of the spirit of the Antichrist as described in Scripture: 'Who is a liar but he that denieth that Jesus is the Christ? He is the antichrist that denieth the Father and the Son' (*1 John* 2:22). Seaver, although an accredited minister of the Anglican Communion was of one mind with Younghusband; in *World Faiths*, the official organ of the World Congress, he wrote:

All formulated religious beliefs, of whatever tradition, are no more than fragmented facets of a central prism, formless and colourless itself, the white light of truth.[6]

If this is true, all formulated beliefs are a hindrance to true religious understanding, and true religious understanding requires that they should be discarded. If, as in the stated aim of the World Congress of Faiths, religion in its normal sense is to be transcended and we are to go beyond all particular expressions of religion, it cannot serve the purpose of religion to maintain one's own particular faith, which the World Congress claimed to encourage people to do. Younghusband's own particular religious stance reveals the impossibility of remaining loyal to any religion while seeking to find an essence common to all.

His blindness to what the Christian gospel was all about is revealed by an episode in his life even more than in his writings. In 1905, he paid two visits to the Welsh revival which had broken out the previous year in the mining village of Brynamman in South Wales through the instrumentality of Rees Howells, which Younghusband described in his book *Modern Mystics* under the title of 'Mass Mysticism'.[7] He tells us it made no immediate impact on him, although he commented that 'In comparison with the singing and the praying at these meetings, the sermons, the music and the prayers of ordinary church people were like thin pipings'.[8] He saw for himself people agonizing in repentance over sin, but it was the resultant joy and exultation which impressed him most: 'all this vast quivering, throbbing, singing, praying, exultant multitude was intensely conscious of the all pervading influence of some invisible reality – now for the first time moving, palpable though invisible in their midst'.[9] He interpreted what he saw in terms of his analysis of mystical experience as an insight into the interconnectedness of the universe dependent on a 'Personality energising, controlling and directing all'.[10]

Younghusband's visit to Wales confirmed his existing views. Its effect on his return home was a brief enjoyment of 'a state of ecstatic exultation' in which he felt 'as if I were in love with every man and woman in the world. All life seemed of one rose-coloured hue and intensely bright . . . All sordidness and baseness was shot through with a radiance that utterly purified their dross. And heaven seemed for the moment established on earth'.[11] His theological assessment of the revival is illuminating: 'As it seems to me, it was this joy and gladness, this holy ecstasy of life, that Jesus was trying to communicate to men rather than any hard and fast doctrines'.[12] What really happened in the revival, the awesome descent of the Holy Spirit of the sovereign God upon men and women in their thousands breaking them with contrition and sweeping them into his kingdom, passed him by.

The World Congress of Faiths expanded rapidly. It came to have branches in France, Belgium, Pakistan, Guyana, and two in India. It can rightly claim to have pioneered the now common inter-faith services. To celebrate the birthday of the Queen, such a service which she attended in person was held on 11 June 1966, in St. Martin-in-the-Fields. In the previous year the Duke of Edinburgh was at a similar service at the opening of the Commonwealth Arts Festival. *World Faiths* (No. 66, Summer 1966) commented:

On these two occasions, both in Anglican Churches, Affirmations of Faith were read by the vicar, followed by readings from the world scriptures, not only by representatives of the Eastern religions and of the Protestant denominations but the Roman Catholics also participated.

These official events are tremendously heartening, the blossoms, perhaps of seeds sown many years ago by this movement and others. *The Times* called the Queen's Birthday Service 'a new departure in multi-religious participation'. But a letter from the Rev Tom Dalton, published in that paper, made it clear that this is nothing new: Beginning, I think, with the Memorial Service for Sir Francis Younghusband in 1942, at St. Martin-in-the-Fields, and 'Every Nation Kneeling', a Service compiled and conducted by the Rev Will Hayes for the World Congress in 1949, All Faith Services have been arranged all over the country and our London one has become an annual event.[13]

Tom Dalton, a Unitarian minister, had been a secretary of the W.C.F., and the Rev Will Hayes was a high-ranking official of the esoteric Order of the Great Companions. The inter-faith movement has affinities with the occult world which will be examined later.

A notable adherent of the W.C.F. was Bishop George Appleton, at one time vicar of St Botolph's Church, Aldgate (1957–1962), later Anglican Archbishop of Jerusalem until his resignation in 1973, and from 1974 to 1978 its chairman. The first inter-faith service in an Anglican Church was held at St. Botolph's during his incumbency in the face of widespread opposition. With a high reputation for spirituality, he nevertheless composed a prayer on the 2,500th anniversary of the Buddha's entry into *Nirvana*, and also wrote a love poem on a Muslim woman saint, Rabia (c. 800 A.D.). As General Secretary of the British Missionary Societies, Appleton regarded it as his task to awaken them to revival of the world religions and to encounter with them.[14] He wrote:

We should try to draw into our fellowship groups that may be on the outer edge of our constituencies, e.g. the more strictly orthodox friends in Judaism, the Orthodox and Evangelical Churches, Muslims, Buddhists, and Hindus and ultimately men of non-faith.[15]

In the same article he suggested that this attempt could be achieved if we concentrated more on God and less on Jesus, a view he repeated at the annual conference of the W.C.F. in 1974:

Do we Christians put Jesus before God, do we let our faith become a stopping point, almost an obstacle to our faith in God? Or do we go with Jesus to God . . . with whom he is eternally present? Are we ready to believe that other people have had experience of the divine and are trying to find their way to God from other starting-points, by whatever name they may call him?[16]

He ignores the fact that until these times Christian proclamation has never so separated God the Father and God the Son; rather the summary of its message was always a call for 'repentance toward God, and faith toward our Lord Jesus Christ' (*Acts 20:21*). This was done on the authority of Jesus himself: 'And this is life eternal, that they may know thee, the only true God, and Jesus Christ, whom thou hast sent' (*John 17:3*). In asking us to dissociate Christ from God, Bishop Appleton is requiring us to take a step which involves disloyalty to Him. Bishop Appleton concluded his address to the annual conference of the W.C.F. in 1975 with the statement:

The battle is a spiritual one. We are beginning to see Truth in all religions – even God in all. Every religion has a mission; *when put together*, they give an idea of the magnificence, the depth and joy of God's total creation.

Thus Appleton begins by removing the emphasis on Jesus, continues by placing it on God from whom he severs Jesus, and ends by removing the emphasis on God to place it on creation. 'Creation spirituality', as it is termed, has proved to be the ultimate goal of the inter-faith movement. This is no new thing; it is the path already followed by unregenerate men in New Testament times (and before). Unregenerate men have always served the creature more than the Creator, who alone is blessed forever (*Rom. 1:25*).

Brief mention has been made of the formation in other countries of bodies with the same aims as the W.C.F. Most significant among these is the 'Temple of Understanding' founded in 1980 in the U.S.A. by Mrs J. Hollister, a Shintoist, which organizes inter-faith gatherings at different venues throughout the world. It enjoys support from the highest quarters. Its early members included Albert Schweitzer, Eleanor Roosevelt, U Thant of the United Nations, Robert McNamara, one time Defence Secretary of the U.S.A. and subsequently head of the World Bank, other holders of high office in the U.S.A. like Chester Bowles and Douglas MacArthur II, and from outside the U.S.A. Dr S. Radhakrishnan, whom we have already met, Sir Roy Welensky of Rhodesia, and the Prime Ministers of New Zealand, Nepal and Morocco. Its religious sponsors included Bishop James A. Pike, Bishop Hanayana, head of the American Buddhist centres, the Unitarian Fellowship, the Society of Friends, the Vedanta Society, the Islamic Conference of Cairo and the United Lodge of Theosophists.

The inclusion of theosophists gives the inter-faith movement a direct contact with the occult world; it has much more than a mere affinity with it. It also has friends in the financial world: John D. Rockefeller IV was among its supporters. By 1963 its membership included six thousand names from the world's great and good, including many Nobel Laureates, drawn from sixty-two countries. Since 1979, the Temple has represented the World Congress of Faiths in the U.S.A. Its first World Spiritual Summit was held in Calcutta in October 1968. The concluding address was given by the Roman Catholic Trappist monk Thomas Merton, the most important advocate of the enrichment which the assimilation of elements from the Eastern religions would bestow on Christianity, who requires a separate consideration which we will give him in due course. Its second summit took place in Geneva from 31 March to 4 April, 1970, and was attended by a hundred and fifty delegates representing fourteen religions. The opening address was given by Dr Carson Blake of the World Council of Churches. An inter-faith service was held in the cathedral of St Pierre, where Anglicans and Roman Catholics worshipped with Buddhists, Hindus, adherents of Jainism, Sikhs, Zoroastrianists, Confucianists and Shintoists. For its fifth summit in October 1975 the Temple chose the cathedral of St John the Divine in New York, which has regularly opened its doors to occultists and New Agers. The main topic discussed was the threats posed to the earth by technology. The inter-faith movement was thus linked with the ecological movement with which it was to develop ever closer connections. The summit was presided over by Jean Houston, a New Ager, who by this time was on the board of the Temple. The Church of Rome had more than one representative. Others who attended were Sir Muhammad Zafrulla Khan, a former President of the International Court of Justice at the Hague and of the U.N. General Assembly, Shimano Eido Roshi, a Zen Buddhist Master, Lord Kosho Ohtani, a Buddhist abbot from Japan, Mrs Birla, a Hindu and chairwoman of the Temple's international committee, Dr Seyyed Hossein Nasr, Director of the Iranian Academy of Philosophy, and Rabbi Robert Gordis, representing Judaism. Hopi and Indian medicine men also participated. Inter-faith services and meditations were held twice a day for four days. For its organizers, the highlight of the summit was a Cosmic Mass:

The most ambitious dramatic event of all was the Cosmic Mass presented five times during the week by the Sufi Order [Sufism is the mystic branch of Islam] with a cast of 300 people. The Cosmic Mass, an extremely elaborate pageant depicting the various evolutionary stages of the world religions and how they may eventually meet on a transcendental plane of universal understanding was written and narrated by Pir Vilayat Inayat Khan, a noted leader of the Sufi Order. At the end of each performance the audience was invited to join in a great dance of celebration and did so with enthusiasm.[17]

After this brief glance at what was happening further afield, we can return to the W.C.F. In 1976, it began to celebrate its founder by an annual Sir Francis Younghusband Memorial Lecture. The lecture of 1986 was delivered by Dr Robert Runcie, then Archbishop of Canterbury, and subsequently available in transcript from Lambeth Palace. After a summary of the experiences of Younghusband and the purposes of his World Congress, and a wide ranging survey of earlier and more recent attitudes of the relationship of the world religions, Dr Runcie affirmed that for Christians the life, suffering, death and resurrection of Jesus would always remain the primary source of knowledge and truth about God; the self-giving of God in his Son was 'firm and fundamental' and 'not negotiable.' He went on to declare that 'other faiths reveal other aspects of God which may enrich and enlarge our Christian understanding.' The implication is clear: the revelation of God in Christ, while it is the primary source of our knowledge of God and is not negotiable, is incomplete and needs to be supplemented. Towards the conclusion of his lecture, Dr Runcie spelled this out explicitly. He quoted the well-known words of Tillich that particular religions are only provisional and need to break through their particularity:

In the depths of every living religion there is a point at which the religion itself loses its importance, and that to which it points breaks through its particularity to a vision of spiritual freedom and to a vision of the spiritual presence in other expressions of the ultimate meaning of man's existence.

For Dr Runcie there can be no question of the finality so magisterially expressed by the writer of the epistle to the Hebrews: 'God, who at sundry times and in divers manners spake in time past unto the fathers by the prophets, hath in these last days spoken unto us by his Son, whom he hath appointed heir of all things, by whom also he made the worlds, who being the brightness of his glory, and the express image of his person, and upholding all things by the word of his power, when he had by himself purged our sins, sat down on the right hand of the Majesty on high' (*Heb. 1:1–3*). If Tillich is correct there can be nothing in any religion which is not negotiable. Dr Runcie cannot have it both ways. He ended with a reference to one of the most prominent secular syncretists, the historian Sir Arnold Toynbee:

The Inter-Faith Movement: A Preliminary Survey

Arnold Toynbee, in a remarkable prophecy, suggested that the present century would be chiefly celebrated by historians hundreds of years hence . . . as the time when the first sign became visible of that great interpretation of Eastern religions and Christianity which gave rise to the great universal religion of the third millennium.

He added that not all would regard such a development as desirable, but did not number himself among such objectors, and without such an explicit repudiation, he must be understood to be endorsing Toynbee's view.

Denying that he was a syncretist ('I am not advocating a single-minded, synthetic model of world religion'), Dr Runcie spoke of 'the moments of revelation' in non-Christian religions and of 'the spiritual treasures which our respective faiths have handed down to us – a spark of divine life and a vision of holiness whereby the lives of countless people in the past and present are nourished, transformed, sustained and sanctified.' Referring to the first meeting of the W.C.F., he identified himself with Younghusband's own words:

Religion, taken as a whole, benefited much from the variety of its different forms. All the centuries that the spirit of God had been working in Christians, he must also have been working in Hindus, Buddhists, Muslims and others. And recognising this important fact, members of the Congress showed no disposition to try to form any new religion: rather were they inclined to draw inspiration from others for the development of their faith.

Younghusband had argued that religious dialogue and shared religious communion made the Hindu 'all the better a Hindu, the Muslim all the better a Muslim, the Christian all the better a Christian'. This contention has since been reiterated countless times, but those who have repeated it have never shown how it is so, and Younghusband's own understanding of Christianity was not benefitted by his contact with other religions, a fact which gives the lie to his thesis. Against the disclaimer quoted by Dr Runcie, we must set his vision of 'a far greater religion yet to be', which though it could not be manufactured artificially, must in the nature of things eventually evolve.

There are two types of syncretism. For a definition of the first, we can turn to the Autumn 1970 issue of *World Faiths*, in which Dr Bishop of the Washington State University wrote:

A second type of monodeism appeared on the scene toward the end of the nineteenth century under the name of syncretism. The intent of its advocates was to create a single world religion by taking the best elements from each religion and fusing them into one or picking out what is unique in the different faiths, and making one religion out of them. The new religion, since it would contain elements of every religion would be universally acceptable.[18]

The definition of the second is given by Dr Visser't Hooft, in his book *No Other Name: The Choice between Syncretism and Christian Universalism*, written while he was General Secretary of the World Council of Churches:

The word syncretism should be reserved for another type of religious attitude, which deserves to have its own name because it is such an important, persistent and widespread religious phenomenon. This is the view that there is no unique revelation in history, that there are many different ways to reach the divine reality, that all formulations of religious truth or experience are by their nature inadequate expressions of that truth and that it is necessary to harmonize as much as possible all religious ideas and experiences so as to create one universal religion for mankind. Professor Oepke puts the matter clearly: 'Real syncretism is always based on the presupposition that all positive religions are only reflections of a universal original religion ("Urreligion") and show therefore only gradual differences.'[19]

Younghusband and all the spokesmen of the W.C.F. whose words we have examined assign revelatory status to all religions and regard each as inadequate on its own. They are syncretists of this second type. So is Dr Runcie with his belief that there are moments of revelation in all faiths, and that the Christian religion needs to be supplemented by their insights into aspects of God which do not come into its view.

Such is the contemporary fascination of the West with the East that there is one passage in Dr Runcie's lecture where Christianity appears as a poor relation to Hinduism:

There were the marvellous early Hindu sculptures at Mahabalipuram, near Madras, where gods and goddesses take hundreds of different forms and images. The sheer diversity of the divine was disconcerting. God seemed somehow greater than western monism.

Dr Runcie thus fails to appreciate the fact that the Christian Scriptures, though a revelation of one God, show that God to be multifaceted. To him, that revelation is clearly inadequate. He patently shares Tillich's view that no one religion affords a complete revelation of God:

We have already begun, painfully, to emancipate ourselves from the isolation which limits religion to the insights and errors of one stream of tradition . . . Was it Max Muller who urged that in respect of religion, 'He who knows one, knows none'?

How he can regard Hinduism with its pantheon of gods, each with its own image, as a divine revelation, when the God of Scripture expressly forbids the making of images (*Exod. 20:4–5*) is a mystery which the God of the Bible, the only true God, alone can understand.

The belief that the Spirit of God has always been at work in all the religions of the world runs counter to the words of Jesus himself, who promised the Holy Spirit only to his followers:

I will pray the Father, and he shall give you another Comforter, that he may abide with you forever, even the Spirit of truth; whom the world cannot receive, because it seeth him not, neither knoweth him (*John 14:16–17*).

Akin to the view that finds the Holy Spirit at the heart of all religions, and as commonly voiced by the proponents of inter-faith activity, is the concept that religion is a manifestation of a spark of divine life in the heart of the believer. This again is contrary to the biblical analysis of men as 'alienated from the life of God through the ignorance that is in them, because of the blindness of their hearts' (*Eph. 4:18*).

Dr Runcie was specially impressed by the well-known invocation of the Upanishads, 'Lead me from the Unreal to the Real, from the Darkness to Light, from Death to Immortality', which he described as 'a prayer of profound longing and hope'. Here for once is a statement from which we need not demur. All through history man has sought God, has looked for the source, purpose and meaning of his own life, and striven for the forgiveness of his sins and for immortality. But it does not require the work of the Holy Spirit to set him on this quest, nor does his search issue from a spark of the divine life within him. It is enough that man was made in the image of God which he retains, because it was not obliterated by the fall, although it was impaired. Man has not ceased to be man, and God has not left man anywhere without a witness to Himself, the witness of his conscience (*Rom. 2:15*). Man still has a limited capacity to distinguish between good and evil, truth and falsehood, purity and impurity, justice and injustice, and compassion and cruelty. But when man fell, he fell under the power of the father of lies, the deceiver who has disguised himself as an angel of light (*John 8:44; 2 Cor. 11:14*), who is also the prince of this world (*John 12:31*). The nobility and apparent holiness of man's religions therefore have a double source – the remnant of the image of God in man, and the activity of Satan. This book is not a study of comparative religion, though as it develops we will need to give some consideration to the teachings of other faiths. Here it is sufficient to point out that Hinduism is primarily monistic. The outer world is *maya*, illusion, and all the diverse things that we perceive are one and the same. The soul of consciousness within man is identical with God. Hinduism is also pantheistic. It argues that everything is one and the one is also divine. The Hindu has no sooner prayed his prayer, 'Lead me from death to immortality', than he makes an about turn, and in place of immortality he seeks annihilation, the annihilation of being absorbed into the ocean of the All-One, or the One-All. Hinduism teaches that the search for immortality is based on the illusory assumption of the reality of the individual. Dr Runcie is wrong. It is not Christianity, with its distinction between the Creator and the creature, which is monistic, but Hinduism.

In accordance with the developments and thinking we have been considering, the annual services for the observance of Commonwealth Day, which for some time have been held in Westminster Abbey, have taken a completely inter-faith character. The service of 1990 began, after the entry of the heads of the Commonwealth organizations and religious leaders, followed by the Queen and Prince Philip, with a reading from the Sutta-Nipata, a discourse of the Buddha about attaining *Nirvana*, the Buddhist concept of salvation, which is akin to that of Hinduism and has nothing in common with that of Christianity. After this, the High Commissioner for Mauritius read from the Svetavatara Upanishad, a Hindu text focusing on Brahma, the supreme god of the Hindu pantheon. Next came a reading from the Qur'an by the High Commissioner for Pakistan of a passage exulting the virtues of Allah. A little later, some schoolgirls read the Prayer for Peace, the words of which are adapted from the Upanishads and often printed in the form of a mandala, a Hindu and Buddhist meditation circle. For the concluding prayers, representatives of the world faiths, together with leaders from the Free Churches, the Church of Scotland and the Roman Catholic Church sat on a stage in the heart of the Abbey. What happened next has been described by a witness, the Rev Tony Higton of Emmanuel Church, Hockley, Essex:

Firstly, the venerable Dr Mebagama Vajiragnana (a Buddhist monk with saffron robe and shaved head) chanted (in Pali) praise to the Buddha, dear to gods and men – who brings the truth. Later Swami Bhavyanada (a robed Hindu holy man) chanted (in Sanskrit) a prayer to Brahma. The Sheikh Mahmoud Hammad (a Muslim leader) chanted praise to Allah 'whom alone we worship'. Soon afterwards Professor Harmindar Singh (a Sikh Leader) chanted (in Punjabi) to God the true Guru 'who is everywhere and in everyone'. The name of Jesus was mentioned only briefly at the end of two prayers (led by the Free Church and Church of Scotland ministers). The Roman Catholic's prayer did not use the name of Jesus, nor did the hymns, affirmation or blessing.[20]

After making representations to the Dean of Westminster and to Dr Runcie without success, Mr Higton wrote to the Queen, since the Abbey lies directly under her responsibility, equally to no effect. Mr Higton organized a petition, which included the words, 'We believe the worship of non-Christian deities in those Observances to be incompatible with the Christian Faith and contradict the fundamental Christian doctrine that Jesus is the only way to God and the only Saviour'. He requested that the Commonwealth Observances should be specifically and solely Christian. At her coronation the Queen pledged herself on oath to maintain to the utmost of her power to 'maintain in the United Kingdom the Protestant reformed religion established by law'. This petition obtained almost seventy thousand signatories, many from sixteen black countries. Christians everywhere know

17

that it is not imperialistic or racist to insist on the uniqueness of Christianity. But the petition also proved ineffective, and the Commonwealth Day Observances continue as before.

On 10 March, 1992, *The Times* reported:

Sheikh Zahran Ibrahim, of the Islamic Cultural Centre and the London Central Mosque, read from the Qur'an. Dr John Rayner, representing the Jewish community, read from the Mishnah Sanhedrin, Professor Harmindar Singh, Secretary of the Sikh Divine Fellowship, read from the Guru Granth Sahib, the Ven Dr Pandith M. Vajiragnana, Head of The London Buddhist Vihera, read from the Sutta-Nipata, a Discourse of the Buddha, and the Rev Swami Bharyandandra, of the Ramakrishna Vedanta Centre, read from the Bhagavad-Gita.

Pupils from the Royal Russell School, Croydon, said the prayer for peace. The name of Jesus was mentioned briefly twice ('Jesus said . . .'; 'Jesus said . . .'). In the 1993 Observance, the first hymn was 'Praise, my soul, the King of Heaven', a safe theocentric hymn, not a potentially divisive Christocentric hymn. There were Jewish, Muslim, Sikh, Buddhist and Hindu readings. The latter affirmed that a good man was born of heaven, thus contradicting the gospel. Jesus again got two mentions, in a reading from Luke 5, beginning 'Jesus said', introducing a passage about not judging, with no reference to the heart of the gospel, the atonement. The second mention was in the prayer of the Roman Catholic representative.[21]

The history of Westminster Abbey between 1902 and today epitomizes the change which has taken place. In 1902 in the rose window of the south transept Jesus occupies the central position, but there are now annual occasions when he is pushed to the periphery, which can only mean he is no longer at the centre of the thinking of the Abbey on any occasion. To them Jesus is one saviour among many; otherwise they would not allow the use of the Abbey for the Commonwealth Day Observances in the form which they have come to take. If Jesus is not Lord of all our time, he is not Lord of any of our time.

The Commonwealth Observances are not the only occasions when Christ has been belittled in Westminster Abbey. On Good Friday, 1994, its Chapter replaced the traditional three hours devotion with a mime enacting the life of a Mexican artist who has become a cult figure in his nation. Before a twenty-foot effigy representing Christ, the actor playing the part of the Mexican hero lay on the floor of the nave until his 'miraculous' resurrection. The Vice-Dean of the Abbey suggested that the artist was 'one of the small lights which has burnt to redeem the darkness of our history'. This implies that there is a process of redemption in human history independent of the redemption achieved once for all at Calvary. The Dean later explained, 'We felt that we should try to draw in casual visitors and tourists, many of whom did not know it was Calvary'. An opportunity of showing them the meaning of Calvary was thus thrown away. Further, the substitution of an ordinary human being for Christ implicitly assumes that Christ is not the only incarnation.

The inter-faith movement is here to stay. From 28 August to 5 September 1993, the second World Parliament of Religions was held, like the first, in Chicago to celebrate its centenary. It included Baha'is, Buddhists, Confucianists, Hindus, Jains, Jews, native American Indians, members of the African Yoruba cult, Sikhs, the Fellowship of Isis, the Covenant of the Goddess, the Earth Spirit Community and the Centre for Women, the Earth and the Divine. These met with representatives of the Presbyterian, Baptist, Methodist and the Anglican, Roman Catholic and Orthodox Churches. It opened with a number of 'blessings' from a variety of religious sources. One of these was given by a High-Priestess of the Temple of Isis, 'in the name of the 10,000 names, the spirits, the birds, the reptiles and trees'. Seminar titles included 'Euthanasia', 'Humanism – The Modern Alternative to Traditional Religion', 'Christian Reflections on the Bhagavad-Gita', 'Spirometry – the Scientific Step towards God', 'The Role of the High-Priestess in the Temple of Isis' and 'The Role of the Goddess'. The witchcraft-based Covenant of the Goddess organized a Full-Moon ritual in Chicago's Grand Park. The Parliament met in a very different climate from that of 1893. While Edward White Benson, the Archbishop of Canterbury, had refused to attend a century ago, the delegates in 1993 received a message of welcome from his successor, Dr George Carey, who believed:

Few things are more important to our world today than the growth of mutual respect and understanding between different faith communities.[22]

There were few Christian dissentients. The Greek Orthodox diocese of Chicago withdrew on 30 August on the ground that it was inconceivable for Orthodox Christianity to establish a perceived relationship with groups which possessed no belief in God or a supreme Being. On the other hand, an Orthodox priest declared in a seminar on 'Shamanism in West Texas', 'It is good to study the Fundies [i.e. the fundamentalists a pejorative term applied to all the groups united by their loyalty to biblical Christianity] so that you will know your enemy'. One of the main lectures was entitled 'A Proposal to Evolve the Parliament toward a United Nations of Religions'. Dr Robert Muller, a United Nations executive, who is active in both the inter-faith movement and the New Age, and whose acquaintance we shall make in the fifth chapter of this study, called for the establishment of a permanent World Council of Religions by 1995. Dr David Ramage, who chaired the parliament, saw the next step as setting up inter-faith centres in key religions of the world and networking relationships between them. The establishment of a global religious council within the next few years was seen as a very real possibility. An article in *Sunrise*, the official journal of the Theosophical Society, a co-sponsor of the Parliament, spoke of it as heralding a climate of world thought 'so that those having leadership responsibilities in the 21st Century will banish intolerance from every phase of human experience'.[23] One acute observer of the parliament commented, 'By ignoring mutually exclusive claims about the personal God and stressing. . . good works by issuing the Global Ethic Document [its one practical achievement], the Parliament may have unwittingly set up a litmus test for the validity of religion – a sort of "religious correctness".'[24] It is not likely that biblical Christianity would pass such a test.

Shortly after the Parliament, the Inter-Faith Association of Edinburgh held a celebration on 23 October, 1993, to commemorate it. Prayers and greetings were sent by Muslim, Buddhist, Hindu, Baha'i and Jewish delegates. The participants were summoned to its sessions by a fanfare of Tibetan horns. It concluded with the presentation of an inter-faith drama by Lothian schoolchildren. The possibility for such an occasion had already been prepared in the preceding May by the General Assembly of the Church of Scotland's rejection of a resolution to affirm 'the teaching of Scripture that Jesus Christ, the incarnate, crucified and risen Son of God is the only Saviour of men and women' and to 'restate the Church of Scotland's commitment to worldwide evangelism'.

The Inter-Faith Association of Edinburgh is only one of many such bodies throughout Britain. Many cities and towns, especially those with a population containing varied ethnic groups, have one. Thirty are affiliated to the Inter-Faith Network for Great Britain, which is in touch with thirty more and hopes to bring all local groups together to form a nationwide body. The aim of the Network is to promote inter-faith dialogue, but its activities also include services of inter-faith worship. It calls for a radical change of approach to mission, which it does not outlaw, although it imposes restrictions on it:

The attempt to convert a committed member of another faith inevitably implies a judgement that the other faith is mistaken or, at the very least, inadequate by comparison with the missionary's own faith. It may consequently be experienced as a disrespectful dishonouring of what that faith holds most sacred and most dear.[25]

'Dialogue' is to be preferred to proselytism, because in it the missionary will come to recognize the spiritual resources which other religions have to offer.

The new attitude to the non-Christian religions which the inter-faith movement has produced is encapsulated in the remarks of the Prince of Wales in his television interview with Jonathan Dimbleby on 29 June, 1994, reported in *The Times* the following day. After the unexceptionable statement that he regarded Muslims and Zoroastrians and all other classes of subject as of equal importance to the throne, clearly referring to them in their role as citizens, he went on to say that he preferred to think of the monarchy as defending 'Faith' and wished the sovereign's role could be described by such a title as 'Defender of the Divine', not 'Defender of the Faith'. The latter meant 'just one particular interpretation of the Faith'; the former was more appropriate since 'We are all actually aiming for the same ultimate goal'.

We may conclude this chapter with a summary of an address given by the Rev Alan Race, Editor of *World Faiths Encounter*, the new title of *World Faiths*, the organ of the W.C.F., on 13 November, 1993. The occasion was a seminar held by World Goodwill, a New Age organization of which we shall have to take notice later in these pages. Alan Race's subject was 'The Inter-Faith Movement, Challenges and Opportunities for the 21st Century'. He started from the premise that it 'will not be enough in the future to live out of one tradition alone. We have entered an era when that attitude has become inadequate in relationship to the interdependent world which we are becoming'. Christianity, that is to say, will be unable to meet the needs of man in the twenty-first century. Religion, he explained, has three elements, spiritual, ethical and philosophical/theological. Part of each aspect is peculiar to a particular faith, but there is a point in each faith where the aspects overlap. This can be discovered as in 'silent waiting' we listen with respect to the faiths of others, which will allow them to accept us as 'welcome guests' and enable us all to enjoy a 'shared experience'. A process of mutual dialogue will result in the mutual transformation of us all. All religions are based on human experience (notice the absence of any reference to revelation), a view we shall meet again when we consider the academic theologians who support inter-faith. They also make a distinction 'between ultimate-reality-in-itself and ultimate-reality-as-filtered-through-cultural-and-historical-lenses'.

Whether human beings are limited to a single life or have before them the prospect of many reincarnations belong to the questions to 'which we can never know the answers'. (This in spite of Hebrews 9:27). Certainty in religious truth is unattainable, yet the twenty-first century holds in store for us 'immense possibilities' of 'a new era in religious understanding', in which 'the religious other' will be seen as inextricably part of our own identity.

While leaders of the inter-faith movement are thus willing to address New Age audiences, New Age publications report with interest inter-faith events. The *World Goodwill Newsletter*,

No. 3, 1994, informs us of a World Congress of Spiritual Concord held in the foothills of the Himalayas at Rishikesh in December, 1993, attended by two hundred people from different faiths and countries, taking the form of a 'meditative working week . . . to concentrate on prayer and meditation, on worship and adoration of the Transcendent, according to a dozen or so of our various religious and spiritual traditions of humanity'. It issued an appeal to 'all interested in the healing of humanity'. People of goodwill were called upon to renew themselves 'not only ethically, but also in their cultural, religious and spiritual roots, so that the light may dawn in ourselves and in the outside world'. They were further exhorted to 'cleanse our institutions and social structures . . . by the gentle but firm power of goodness in action, developed through prayer and meditation'. All this without reference to him who is the Light of the world.

After this general survey, we turn to a more rigorous investigation of the theology underpinning the inter-faith movement.

CHAPTER II

Pluralists and Syncretists:
The Theologians and Inter-Faith

1 : *The Pluralists*

The inter-faith movement has produced a vast body of literature which it is impossible to survey in this brief study. But all of the arguments in its favour are conveniently presented in *The Myth of Christian Uniqueness*, edited by John Hick and Paul F. Knitter, which contains papers read at a colloquy held at the Claremont Graduate School, Claremont, California, 7–8 March 1986. The contributors were all distinguished academic theologians, who held a position they termed 'pluralism', which has come to be more common than 'inter-faith'. In his preface Knitter distinguishes between three positions which may characterize the Christian attitude to other religions: (i) the conservative exclusivist approach which maintains that salvation is to be found only in Christ; (ii) the liberal inclusivist attitude which recognizes other religions as salvific in nature, but regards the salvific element as the result of Christ's redemptive work and needing to be fulfilled in him; (iii) the pluralist position which abandons all insistence on the superiority or finality of Christ and Christianity and recognizes the independent saving validity of other faiths.[1]

In studying *The Myth of Christian Uniqueness* we need not study each paper as it stands. It will be clearer to summarize them thematically. A basic contention of all the contributors is that all religions are historically conditioned, the product of a particular culture at a particular time, and reflecting its limitations as well as its insights, rather than being grounded in divine revelation. This is different from the view of Dr Runcie that every religion contains revelatory moments. Aloysius Pieris, S.J., in his paper on 'The Buddha and the Christ: Mediators of Liberation', goes so far as to say that the core of every religion is a human

27

experience, which is kept alive and made available to successive generations by the collective memory of that experience. Every religion would die as soon as it was born if it did not devise some means of perpetuating the experience and making it accessible to succeeding generations by a system of symbols, rites and beliefs.[2] This means that Christians keep Christianity alive, Hindus keep Hinduism alive and Muslims keep Islam alive. Whatever is the case with Hinduism and Islam, it is certainly not the case with Christianity. Christ guaranteed the perpetuity of his church on the basis of his identity as the Son of God (*Matt. 16:16–17*). Certainly his followers would have their part in its continuance (*John 17:20*), but their labours and the ultimate survival of the church and the salvation of its members would rest on his ongoing activity as intercessor (*Heb. 7:25*). Such claims were never made by Mohammed or the Buddha and are not found in the Hindu scriptures.

The contention that religions are historically conditioned calls into question the status of revelation, particularly of the Christian revelation with its claim to uniqueness and finality. If Christian insights and values are the products of a historical development and not grounded directly in divine revelation, they may not completely lose their point, but the conviction of their absoluteness no longer holds good. This is the thesis of Gordon D. Kaufman in his contribution to the colloquy, 'Religious Diversity, Historical Consciousness and Christian Theology'.[3] John Hick in 'The Non-Absoluteness of Christianity' accordingly argues that the claim that Christianity has a power to transform human life in a way that no other religions possess must be demonstrated empirically, from the facts of history.[4] He continues by asserting that this cannot be done: 'We have no good grounds for maintaining that Christianity has produced or is producing more saints, in proportion to population, or a higher quality of saintliness, than any other of the great streams of religious life'.[5] A Christian theology informed by a thoroughgoing historical consciousness is not in a position to assert that its assertions are directly and uniquely informed and authorized by divine revelation.[6] Yet another contributor, Langdon Gilkey, declares that the creeds and confessions of Christianity and even the words of Scripture themselves must be seen as human, and therefore as the relative expressions of a truth that transcends any single expression of it. To defend them is not to defend God, and is morally dubious.[7] Wilfred Cantwell Smith continues the theme: to claim that only Christianity is true, final and salvific constitutes idolatry, and a religious form of imperialism. We are to understand that He/She/It inspired us to construct it, just as He/She/It inspired Muslims to construct Islam and so on.[8] To some pluralists it is a matter of indifference whether God is describe in masculine, feminine, or impersonal terms.

It is further argued that through the incarnation God 'relativized himself' in history: Christians should therefore ask themselves whether they are justified in absolutizing him in doctrine.[9] But though Christ limited himself in becoming man (*Phil. 2:5–8*), he did not relativize himself and he made absolute claims. More than one contributor suggests that in view of the incomprehensible nature of the ultimate divine Reality, the central 'symbols' of God and Christ and the Christian concept of revelation do not need to be interpreted more liberally: they may have to be discarded altogether.

The contributors to *The Myth of Christian Uniqueness* believe that the faith that God became incarnate only in Jesus Christ may be rejected without hesitation and without further consideration. According to Hick, to speak of God's love becoming incarnate is to speak of men and women in whose lives God's grace has moved so effectively that they have become instruments of his purpose on earth. Every man may constitute a locus of divine incarnation. Incarnation has occurred in many different ways and degrees and persons. Whether it has occurred more fully in one case than in others, or even absolutely in Jesus, cannot be determined a priori only on the basis of historical information. This means in practice that the issue cannot be settled, for we have no evidence in the Gospels about Jesus' inner or outer life to entitle us to make any judgement on the matter.[10]

In spite of this verdict, one of the contributors, Seiichi Yagi, a leader in Buddhist-Christian dialogue in Japan, attempts to assess the measure to which Jesus was the incarnation of God by analyzing two groups of his recorded sayings, the 'I' sayings and the 'Son of Man' sayings.[11] But he does so on a Buddhist basis, not by any historical criteria, namely, the Buddhist distinction between a primary and a secondary contact of God with the human self. The primary contact is the presence of God within each one of us, a belief which Buddhism shares with Hinduism. The secondary contact is our own awakening to the fact of this presence, which Hinduism terms our realization of God. Thus the Gospels are to be evaluated in the light of concepts which are totally alien to them. Jesus attained to this 'awakening' so completely that, like the Buddha, he became the model for all other selves. The ground of salvation, however, is not the secondary contact, the moment of illumination, but the primary contact, the presence of God within us. Here Christians and Buddhists are on common ground. When Jesus said, 'I say', it was not his empirical self which was speaking, but the 'divine in him'.[12] In the 'Son of Man' sayings Jesus meant to imply that he personified the reign of God, just as Amida Buddha in Pure Land Buddhism personified the saving activity of the Formless from whom he came and which he revealed to his believers.[13] But the 'Son of Man' sayings were interpreted by Jesus' followers, who had not been awakened to God as the ground of their being, as a claim of Jesus to be divine. Jesus, however, did not deify himself for us or hold himself to be divine. Rather, he was aware that his actions were those of the Son of Man, that is, of an awakened and enlightened man within him.[14]

Contrary to Hick, Yagi believes that the New Testament does tell us a lot about the inner life of Jesus, so much, indeed, that it shows us that Jesus was able to distinguish between 'his empirical and his real self'. Yagi believes that the incarnation amounts to the identity, in the depth of the human self, of the divine and the human.[15] Every man, it follows, is an incarnation: all he needs is to become aware of the fact. However difficult it is to speak as Jesus did, it is possible for us all to do so as soon as we are awakened to the God within us.[16]

If this is so, it is a puzzle why those who listened to Jesus were so amazed and impressed by his words (*Luke 4:22; John 7:46*). As a corollary to his analysis, Seiichi Yagi gives us an explanation of the resurrection. This is not to be thought of as bodily: talk of 'resurrection' was the disciples' way of expressing the moment of their illumination, their awakening to the fact of the God within them.[17] Revelation is also to be understood as the moment of this enlightenment, not as something given in the past.[18] Presumably we are offered this interpretation as an example of the way insights from another faith can enrich our Chrisian understanding. We are explicitly told, in fact, that 'our investigation of the New Testament is given a new stimulus and light from dialogue with other world religions'.[19]

Another participant, this time from a Hindu background, Raimundo Panikkar, well known for his *The Hidden Christ of Hinduism* (by which he meant the Christ within Hinduism, hidden not only from Hindus but also from Christians) agrees with this interpretation of the incarnation.[20] If Christians can extricate 'the Christic principle' from their religion, that is, refrain from placing Christ at the centre of their faith, then the incarnation (shorn of an absolute interpretation) will be seen as a dimension present at least potentially in every human being.[21] Further, we can envisage a continuous incarnation, not only in man, but in the being of all creatures (here, Panikkar's Hinduism absorbs his Christian faith and detracts from it rather than enhancing it): 'every being is a *Christophany*'.[22] For Panikkar, Christ is unique as a loved child is unique for its parents.[23] Thus the pluralists align themselves with Sir Francis Younghusband: if Christ is divine other men are potentially divine.

The Christian doctrines of the incarnation and a bodily resurrection, and the Christian view of revelation as something given in the past, are all therefore expendable. So, Hick tells us, is the doctrine of the atonement. Salvation can no longer be defined as inclusion in the scope of the divine pardon made available by Christ's atoning death. He informs us that the theory of atonement to religious pluralists is that of Jesus himself: the prodigal son was forgiven on the sole ground of his repentance. God in no way requires satisfaction for sin, otherwise forgiveness would not be the sheer miracle that Jesus showed it to be.[24] If indeed this is the case, then Hick is right in claiming that the pluralistic vision does not require a departure from the Christian tradition, and its quest for discovering God's presence and activity within other streams of life is justified: 'the resulting perception is not the one and only way of salvation, but one among several'.[25] Unfortunately for the pluralists, Jesus' view of forgiveness was not what Hick says it was. Jesus declared that the

Son of Man came to give his life as ransom for many (*Mark 10:45*), a saying of undoubted authenticity.[26] Without the biblical doctrines, which the pluralists regard as expendable, there is no Christianity. It is not a 'myth' which the pluralists have thrown overboard, but Christianity itself.

We have already seen that the pluralists regard acceptance of the divine inspiration of the Bible idolatrous. They believe that the Hindus and Buddhists have a more appropriate attitude to their own scriptures on which they themselves seem to place a higher value than professed Christians do on their own sacred texts. The Christian 'error' is to emphasize the writtenness of the text. In Eastern religions, by contrast, according to Samartha, the authority of the texts rests on 'hearing and seeing' their words. The words themselves, even their very sound, are holy.[27] Dr Visser't Hooft has aptly commented, 'While all religions are equal, the Vedanta religion is more equal than others'.[28] It does not seem reasonable to elevate the sound of the words above their sense, as Samartha does. In fact, the words of the prophets in the Bible were often spoken to an audience before being written down, with an explicit warning against being captivated by the sound without heeding the message: 'And, lo, thou art unto them as a very lovely song of one that hath a pleasant voice, and can play well on an instrument; for they hear thy words, but they do them not' (*Ezek. 33:32*). Hearing the Word of God and heeding it is more important than its writtenness, but it would not be there to be heard and heeded if it were not written. Mere hearing is of no consequence: what matters is obeying the moral imperative which the Word of God lays upon man. We are enjoined to take heed how we hear (*Luke 8:18*). The sound of words in themselves, whether written or spoken, is of no consequence; it is the content that matters. There is no holiness in a mere sound, and a mere sound has no power to confer holiness.

All these pluralists tell us, as we have in part discovered, that one of the reasons why Christianity must abandon its claim to be the only way to God is that no one religion is adequate to give expression to the infinite Ultimate Reality, whether it be referred to as He, She or It. Distancing ourselves from our Christian tradition, we must take into account the non-personal as well as the personal nature of the Ultimate. The infinite manifests itself in the relativity of each religion, the unconditioned within the conditioned framework of every faith. It may be conceived of as 'God', but the term 'God' must now be understood as symbolic. The unconditioned is transcended by an infinite mystery, pervaded by non-being as well as by being, a mystery relatively manifested as God, but also in other ways and through other symbols, and ultimately as ultimate love. What is here truly apprehended, acknowledged and witnessed to is not only revealed in Christ, but through other media and by means of other symbols, for example, the Bodhisattva (a term in Mahayana Buddhism for one who has earned his own salvation, as Buddhists understand salvation, but who voluntarily renounces it out of compassion for his fellow men to help them to salvation, though it may take innumerable rebirths for him to do so). The Christian revelation, and all other revelations, must be understood in relation to one another in a way that relativizes them all.[29] All are valid, from secular humanism to idolatry.

The term 'idolatry', argues another contributor, betrays a misunderstanding of what the idolater is doing. No one has ever worshipped an idol, but only God in the form of an idol. Idolatry is also a reaching out to the transcendent. The concept of idolatry is an unfortunate legacy which Christianity, together with its claim to exclusiveness, has inherited from Judaism.[30] For the pluralists, Exodus 20:4–5 is no longer valid. In brief, the idea that Christian and biblical faith has a monopoly of religious truth is absurd religious chauvinism. The divine Being that generates, upholds and renews the world is truly universal, and is the father and mother of all peoples without discrimination. True religion and true relationship to the divine is to be found in all religions. 'God/ess is the ground of all being and not just of human beings'.[31]

Samartha, the contributor who spoke of God relativizing himself in history, declares that when alternative ways of salvation have provided meaning and purpose for millions of persons in other cultures for two or three thousand years, to claim that the Judeo-Christian-Western tradition has the only answer to all problems and in all places in the world is presumptuous and incredible. The validity of the Christian experience of salvation is, supposedly, not in question but exclusive claims for it are. Christians must acknowledge their way is only one among many: 'If salvation comes from God – and for Christians it cannot be otherwise – then possibilities should be left open to recognize the validity of other experiences of salvation'.[32] After all these statements, it is not surprising that this same participant should assert that to claim 'that Jesus Christ is God' is to say 'that Jesus Christ is the tribal God of Christians over against the gods of other peoples'.[33] We are not to elevate Jesus to the status of God or to limit the Christ to Jesus of Nazareth.[34] The second of these vetoes raises an important issue which must be discussed at a later stage in this study.

The pluralists do not believe that there are common principles on the basis of which religions can be amalgamated. No one doctrine can be singled out and established as universal in all religions as a point of unity with other traditions. 'God', it is asserted, 'is as similar to – and as different from – the ultimate principles of Hinduism and Buddhism as are Christ and Krishna or Christ and the Bodhisattva'.[35] Philosophy cannot find a way to unite them, because all philosophies are relative and conditioned.[36] Nor can the mystical core at the heart of each religion provide a unifying factor, because its extraction would separate it from the other factors which are essential to a religion, namely, its concepts of morality, its sacraments and its liturgy. In every case, the extraction of the mystical element for the sake of unity would therefore bring it into an alien framework.[37] Accordingly, we must accept each particular religion as it is as both true and relative, a true revelation for a particular community, but relative when placed side by side with the true revelations of other communities, and relative in relationship to the Absolute which each partially and distortedly manifests.[38]

If this is the case, it may legitimately be asked how inter-religious dialogue is possible, and what can be gained from it. Plurality implies parity: each religion, though incomplete in its relativity, is equally valid. Basically, the attitude of the pluralists to religion is that of Hinduism. There are different *margas*, or paths, suitable for the aptitudes of different peoples. The Hindu emphasis, and that of the pluralists, is on the mystery, the transcendent centre greater than our apprehension of it, and the sum total of our apprehensions, a mystery which is beyond the theistic–non-theistic debate. There is diversity within the heart of Being itself, and therefore within the human heart. There are accordingly different ways of salvation, and different disciplines to achieve it.

In spite of the irreducibility of religions to a common essence, inter-religious dialogue is necessary. In the modern world, the solution of urgent human problems is more important than weighing the truth claims of the various faiths. One of the advantages of inter-faith encounter and dialogue, Dr Runcie told us in his Younghusband Memorial Lecture, was that it helped us 'to avoid making crude choices between what is "true" and what is "false" in various religions'. The pluralists would concur; their assumption (and it is an assumption) that all religions without exception are relative and inadequate does indeed make assessing their truth claims a crude procedure. A strong pragmatic note was sounded throughout the whole colloquy. There are more urgent questions than the question of religious truth. The third section of *The Myth of Christian Uniqueness* is given over to the discussion of 'The Ethico-Practical Bridge: Justice'.[39] There is the threat of a nuclear holocaust, and the whole world is contaminated by the plague of oppression and injustice. There is the third world, and women everywhere are among the non-persons. (Two of the participants argued the feminist case). Religions can only make a contribution to the solution of all these practical difficulties if they act together. If they wait to find out what they have in common, action will be delayed. The pressing need is for a global ethic, and the task is too great to be accomplished by any one nation, culture or religion. If there is no common ground or essence between religions, the needs of the world should provide them with a common approach and context for joint action. The pluralists say that when Christians concentrate on the nature of Christ, as they did in the early centuries of their history, they ignore his lordship and neglect the mission they share with him, of transforming the world 'psycho-spiritually and socio-politically' into his kingdom of peace and justice.[40] According to Paul Knitter, identification with the poor is the first step in understanding the Bible.[41] *Praxis*, right action, is always the heart of Christianity: we cannot know who Jesus is unless we are following him by placing his message at the centre of our lives.[42] The recognition of the primacy of right action over right doctrine could bring Christians into the salutary realization that if claims about the finality of Christ are not presently possible, they might ultimately not be necessary.[43] In any event, the right practice of working for Christ's kingdom is more important than right knowledge concerning the nature of God or Jesus himself.[45]

While Christians through this liberation theology are 'discovering' God's preferential option for the poor, the social dimensions of Buddhism and Hinduism are contemporaneously being rescued from oblivion by adherents of those faiths. One of the titles of the Buddha implies his compassionate involvement with the liberation of all human beings, and the Hindu Vinobe Bhave is well known for his leadership of a movement for land reform in India. Thus the humanitarian concern of most religions is held to provide an existing basis for common action, it makes inter-religious dialogue possible, and it may ultimately reveal to the different religions that they have been following a common path all the time. Raimundo Panikkar speaks of 'Christianness', which he defines as adopting a Christ-like attitude without necessarily having a personal faith in Christ. Such an attitude may grow out of Christian faith but it transcends it. It is more in evidence in Latin America, the home of liberation theology, than in the rest of Christianity.

To be universally effective, liberation theology, which is based on Western thought, needs the help of Asian religions.[46] It must speak up not only on behalf of the poor, but also on behalf of womankind, for in traditional Christianity women appear only in the margin as sinners and the repentant recipients of grace (a strange statement in the light of the scriptural inclusion of men as well as women in this category: 'All have sinned and come short of the glory of God', (*Rom. 3:23*). The advocates of pluralism are without exception advocates of feminism. What they end by producing is a new version of the social gospel, a global and inter-faith social gospel, embracing the oppressed everywhere. Knitter argues that it is the soteriologies of the great faiths as well as their humanitarian concerns which lead them into commitment to the poor and to the non-person, but he redefines

soteriology so that it is no longer soteriology, the doctrine of how
man may be reconciled to God, but a secular process, the process
of 'humanization', thus limiting it to the dimension of what Hans
Küng terms the 'humanum'.[47] The 'humanum' must be exten-
ded to include human beings all over the globe, since there are so
many areas of the globe where human beings are not treated as
human. What is needed is a 'planetarian consciousness'.[48]

One more work requires consideration because of the eminence of its author, Hans Küng, namely *Global Responsibility: In
Search of a World Ethic*. Küng is not strictly a pluralist, but his
views have something in common with those of Raimundo
Panikkar. In this book he addresses himself to the same
problems, and even a brief survey of inter-faith thinking requires
a consideration of his position in view of this theological
eminence and of the widespread influence of his earlier book, *On
Being a Christian Today*. He would certainly distance himself
from the pluralist contention that the central Christian symbols
of God and Christ may ultimately have to be discarded. He
declares at the outset that Christians can never renounce the
normativeness and finality of Christ, though his conclusion is not
fully consistent with this assertion. The main thrust of *Global
Responsibility: In Search of a World Ethic*, however, strikes the
same pragmatic note prominent in the pluralists. In the preface,
we read one pithily expressed contention: 'No survival without a
world ethic. No world peace without peace between the religions. No peace between the religions without dialogue between the religions'.[49] Towards the close, we encounter the same
conviction couched in almost the same phraseology: 'No human
life together without a world ethic for the nations: no peace
among the nations without peace among the religions: no peace
among the religions without dialogue among the religions'.[50]

A considerable part of Küng's book is given up to a description
of the world predicament. We have, he says, science without
wisdom, technology without the spiritual energy to bring it
under control, industry blind to ecological needs, and democracy
without the moral principles to cope with the vested interests of
the individuals and groups holding power. We need an ethically
responsible society instead of one that has thrown off all
restraints, a technology which seeks to serve rather than to

dominate, an industry which does not destroy the environment but furthers the interests of mankind in accordance with nature, and a democracy which is no mere legal form but which is lived out. These ends may be brought about by a coalition of believers and non-believers, who must both learn to live and think in a global context and combine the intellectualism of Europe and America with the intuitionism of Asia.

But although the unbeliever can live an authentically moral life, Küng believes, he cannot ultimately give a reason for doing so. Morality needs the underpinnng of religion, which alone can communicate an all-embracing horizon of meaning. The secular world has tried to banish religion, but religion nevertheless remains a universal phenomenon and cannot be eliminated. Without religion, the current need to restrain the power which technology has given us and to control our own consumerism for the benefit of the future cannot be met. Religions offer a vision of the meaning of everything in the light of an ultimate reality. In the last analysis, only the Unconditional can impose an unconditional obligation, and only the Absolute can be absolutely binding.

All religions should therefore find themselves in the fight against the vices of the world and in the encouragement of world virtue. This should be possible because on all major ethical issues the teaching of the world religions is the same, and each also has its own valuable contribution to make. For example, Buddhism with its emphasis on contentment and lack of envy, and Islam with its sense of order and striving for justice. Here Küng cites the World Conference for Justice and Peace held at Kyoto, Japan in October, 1970, where Christians met on equal terms with Buddhists, Jains, Hindus, Jews, Shintoists, Muslims, Sikhs, Zoroastrians and representatives of a considerable number of the animist religions. All shared the conviction of the unity of the human race and of the dignity of the individual, the belief that love, compassion, unselfishness, inner truth and the hope that the good would ultimately prevail, and acknowledged the obligation to stand with the poor against the oppressor. Perhaps doctrinal considerations were not the issue at this conference; its principal themes were disarmament, human rights and development. The opening address given by a Buddhist was a warning against the danger of a nuclear holocaust. It is significant, however, that the speech of Dr Carson Blake, the General Secretary of the World Council of Churches received the hearty approval of Sir Muhammad Zafrulla Khan, President of the International Court of Justice at the Hague and of the seventeenth session of the United Nations: 'Dr Blake did not stress any single value which I, as Muslim, could not wholly endorse'.[51] Yet for all its secular concerns, it was an occasion for inter-faith worship. The conference began with prayer by four Buddhist priests. Kyoto constituted a new landmark in the inter-faith movement, but since Küng singles it out for special mention, this seems a more appropriate place to bring it to notice than our brief preliminary survey.

Though he shares the pragmatic concerns of the pluralists, Küng is not so dismissive of the truth claims of the religions as some of them. This question cannot be set aside. He identifies three positions it is possible to adopt, none of which offers a solution. The first he terms the fortress strategy: one's own religion is true, the others false. The second is the strategy of playing down the differences: each religion has its own truth, so there is no problem. But the argument that anything goes does not hold good; it cannot answer the basic human questions about truth and meaning. Thirdly, there is the strategy of embrace: all historical religions are part of the one true religion, all empirical religions are stages in the evolution of a universal religion. In support of this view, appeal is made to what the pluralists term the mystic core of religion. The outcome of the strategy would be the integration of the religions by denying their identity, an outcome no religion wishing to remain true to itself could allow. But there is, he thinks, a fourth and viable strategy, namely, a critical comparison of one's own religion with others and a critical reflection of the history of its failures, which would raise the question of a universal criterion of truth and goodness applicable to all religions. The boundaries of truth and untruth run through one's own, so that criticism of another can be justified only by self-criticism. Each religion needs a mirror to be held up to it by other religions.

Religions must therefore enter into dialogue with one another for their own sake as well as for the sake of humanity. Such dialogue would require steadfastness to one's own religion. There can be no indifferentism in which every religion is of equal value, and equally there can be no alleged orthodoxy making itself a criterion for universal truth. A relativism for which there is no Absolute must give way to a sense of relativity which recognizes the relativity of all human input into religion. Küng does not deal with the issue of revelation, except to rule out an appeal to the Bible as inappropriate. A syncretism where everything possible and impossible is mixed and fused is also out of place. Instead there must be a will for synthesis which would result in a process of growing together in the face of oppositions and antagonisms so that peace can prevail between different cultural landscapes, none remaining the same, but changing with the landscape, each bringing water from an internal source. All respond to the same basic human questions about the purpose of life and the basis of moral awareness, offering similar ways out of the distress, suffering and guilt of existence through meaningful and responsible action in this life to an abiding and eternal salvation.

Although he contends that the *humanum* must be grounded in the divine, Küng here overlooks divine grace as well as divine revelation. Through the sharing of information and through reciprocal challenges, the world religions will be transformed by a common quest for a greater truth and for the mystery of the one true God, which will only be revealed, if God so wills, at the end of history. Thus Küng's vision is identical with that of Young-husband of a greater religion yet to be. Interestingly, in spite of his stress on steadfastness, and his insistence that Christians can never renounce their own religion in favour of other Christs, part of the transformation he envisages is the transformation of Christology in the light of Muslim insights.[52] He does not enlarge on this point; perhaps he will clarify it in his proposed in-depth study of Islam. But clearly for Küng, as for Dr Runcie, the writer of the epistle to the Hebrews might never have written his declaration of the finality of God's revelation in Christ (*Heb. 1:1–3*). This is a text to which we shall refer again. It means that God has completed his revelation, and in seeking further light from other faiths, the pluralists are ignoring this finality, and seeking revelation where it is not to be found.

The Pluralists

In their emphasis on the divine mystery they ignore the words:

The secret things belong unto the Lord our God: but those things which are revealed belong unto us and to our children for ever (*Deut. 29: 29*).

2: *The Syncretists*

No two individuals have done more for the rapprochement of Christianity and Eastern religions than the English Benedictine monk Dom Bede Griffiths and the American Trappist Thomas Merton. Griffiths, by taking on board elements of Hinduism, and Merton by doing the same with Buddhism, have gone beyond pluralism into the realm of syncretism. They have done so unintentionally. Certainly Griffiths used Hindu thought forms and ceremonial to make Christianity more acceptable to Hinduism, but in doing so he reshaped Christian theology and worship into a guise which was Hindu in some of its aspects. Merton set doctrinal differences on one side on the grounds that all mystical experience has an identical source, thus finding in mysticism an area within which every religion could be encompassed.

Born in 1906 and christened Alan Richard, Griffiths became a pupil of C. S. Lewis at Oxford, with whom he corresponded throughout his life. In his last term at his school, Christ's Hospital, he had an intense mystical experience induced by a solitary walk through the playing fields past a hawthorn tree, with a lark singing in flight and the earth covered by the veil of dusk. His consciousness was awakened to a new dimension of existence. This experience of exaltation in the presence of nature was akin to that expressed in the poetry of Wordsworth, and typical of the nature mysticism analysed by R. C. Zaehner in his well-known *Mysticism, Sacred and Profane*. After leaving Oxford, he spent some time in the study of philosophy and in regular Bible reading. It was during this period that he was introduced to the *Bhagavad-Gita*, *The Buddha's Way of Life*, and the sayings of Lao Tzu by a theosophist friend of his mother.

Among the philosophers it was Spinoza who most impressed him by showing him that the power behind the universe was a rational power who could be loved as well as known. Through Spinoza, if at a subconscious level, he was already pointed in the direction of pantheism. By way of contrast, his family had gathered round the piano on Sundays to sing Moody and Sankey hymns. His philosophical and religious search steadily became more religious, and as it did so, the Bible lost its hold on him and he turned to the mystics. He was thus set on the direction his life was to take.

He was received into the Roman Catholic Church in 1932 at the Benedictine monastery of Prinknash, and professed as monk in 1936 with the name 'Bede'. During his time at Prinknash he began the serious study of Chinese and Indian philosophy to which he had already been introduced. In 1955, he set out for India in the company of the Indian Father Benedict Alapatt, who had suggested to the Prinknash monks that a Benedictine foundation should be started there. They established it at Kengeri near Bangalore, and initially adhered to the normal Benedictine life, using its Latin rite, in the belief that no more was required. But impressed from the time of his arrival in India with the conviction that Hinduism was imbued with a deep sense of the sacred, Griffiths could not rest content with his initial step, and in 1958 he moved to Kerala with his companion where near the mountain of Kurisumala he founded an ashram based on the monastic tradition, but adopting an Indian character. Ultimately he settled in Tamil Nadu, a few miles west of Tiruchirappalli on the banks of the sacred river Cauvery, the Ganges of South India, where he founded his Saccidananda Ashram.

Griffiths' initiative had been anticipated by two other Catholic priests, Monchanin and Le Saux, at Shantinavam Ashram established in 1950, also in the region of the Cauvery. To make Christianity more acceptable to the Hindu they adopted the saffron robe of the *sannyasis* (saffron is a symbol of enlightenment because it represents earth illuminated by the sunlight), the holy men of India, who according to Hindu tradition, having fulfilled their duty to God and society in the prime of life, abandoned the world for a solitary wandering life in renunciation of self; dependent completely on charity, they embarked on the quest of Brahman, the Absolute devoid of all attributes in its pure simplicity. This ultimate simplicity of the Absolute they expressed in the formula SACCIDANANDA, a composite term made up from the words SAT (being), CIT (knowledge), and ANANDA (bliss). Monchanin and Le Saux found in it a parallel with the Trinity:

More fervently and with greater appreciation than any of his fellow-sannyasis can the Christian monk utter: SAT, when thinking of the Father, the 'Principleness' Principle, the very source and end of the expansion and 'recollection' of the divine life; CIT, when remembering the eternal Son, the Logos, the Intellectual Consubstantial Image of the Existent; ANANDA, when meditating on the Paraclete, unifying together the Father and the Son.[53]

Griffiths was deeply influenced by Monchanin and Le Saux, whose work he described in *Christian Ashram, Essays towards a Hindu Christian Dialogue*. It was because of the alleged parallel with the Trinity that he gave its name to his ashram. The formula is scattered throughout his writings, often in a general sense to express the approximation of Hinduism to Christianity, but also specifically as an equivalent of the Trinity. But 'Saccidananda' is abstract and impersonal, the Trinity living and personal. It contains nothing of the willingness of the Father to give the Son for man's redemption, the willingness of the Son to obey the Father's purpose, and the loving co-operation of the Spirit in applying the work of divine redemption to the human heart. Nor does it express anything of the personal fellowship which the Christian believer enjoys with each of the persons of the Holy Trinity.

The life at the Saccidananda Ashram has been described by Griffiths' biographer. Five times a day, the community gathers in its temple to meditate with the help of Hindu, Buddhist and Christian prayers. A mass of the Indian rite, going back to the Syrian Church established in India at a very early date, is used, but with the addition of elements reflecting the cosmic symbolism of Hinduism. As in Hindu temples, the worshippers mark their foreheads at different times of the day with coloured powders. In the morning, paste of sandalwood is used to represent the grace of God; at noon, a red powder, *kumkum* is placed on the forehead, marking the third eye which signifies the internal knowledge and intuitive experience of God; in the evening *vibhuti*, ashes are used to symbolize human mortality and the purification of the self by burning away every defilement. The temple itself, in its building and design, reflects all the symbolism of the East. Griffiths himself wears the robe of the sannyasi, the robe of renunciation.

He has expounded his beliefs not only in *Christian Ashram* but also in later books, *Vedanta and Christian Faith* (1973), *Return to the Centre* (1976), *The Marriage of East and West* (1982), *The Cosmic Revelation* (1983), and in lectures and addresses given during his worldwide journeys. Further insight into his thought is afforded by interviews with his biographer.

Griffiths would not regard himself as a syncretist, and syncretism is not his aim. For a Christian, man is made in the image of God, and cannot as in Hinduism be identified with him. Man, secondly, is separated from God not by illusion or ignorance, but by sin, his aversion from the will of God, who is absolute good. Sin therefore cannot be dispelled by enlightenment of knowledge; it is a fault in our nature for which atonement has to be made. The meeting-place of religions can take place only in Christ. Griffiths is convinced that there can be such a meeting-place for Christ is not only the centre and ground of our being, but the point at which we encounter all other men and the whole world of nature:

It is at this point that the meeting of religions must ultimately take place. For here, just as there is neither 'Jew nor Greek', so there is neither Hindu or Buddhist, neither Muslim nor Parsee, but all are one in Christ.[54]

The world, however, needs a new structure and a new spirituality. India, which in this century has produced spiritual geniuses unequalled in the West, has a natural claim to spiritual leadership. This is so in the first place, because Hinduism has retained an interiority which not merely the secular West, with its interest in technology and the manipulation of things, but even the Christian West (so far as it remains Christian) has lost. Griffiths quotes the Kathopanishad:

The self-existent pierced the opening of the senses so that they turned outward; therefore man looks outwards, not within himself. *Some wise man, desiring immortality, turned his eyes inwards and saw the self.*[55]

These words reflect the direction of the Hindu mind throughout its history, a movement of introversion and a turning away from the eternal world to discover the hidden source of Being, the ground of the Self. In the second place, Hinduism, according to Griffiths, constitutes the deepest expression of the primeval revelation of God in nature. Everything in nature is sacred, from the earth and sky to the hills, trees and rivers and above all man himself. The world is not a symbol, but an actual manifestation of God, identical in essence with the divine being. For this reason, Hinduism is not polytheistic and, according to Griffiths, not even idolatrous; every god is a manifestation of the one absolute Being, and every idol a representation of the one infinite Spirit. The Hindu temple, with its walls decorated with figures of animals and gods, leads one from the outward appearance of life in this world to the central shrine, the *garbha griha*, representing the 'cave of the heart', containing only a bare stone, a symbol of the formless divinity, the absolute godhead, which is beyond all 'name and form'.[56] Through contemplation, the soul realizes in a mystical experience in the ultimate ground of all being its unity with the Brahman, the ultimate ground of all being, expressed in the formula TAT TWAM ASI – Thou art That.

The difficulty of any consideration of Hinduism is that it is not a monolithic religion. Beginning with the *Vedas* before 600 B.C., we find the worship of many gods through ritual sacrifice. Towards the end of the Vedic period, Hinduism turned its interest from the plurality of gods in an attempt to discover the power of which they were the manifestation, the unifying principle of the universe. Thus we come to the development of the *Vedanta*, which Griffiths regards as the greatest system of natural theology the world has known. It was developed over a period of two thousand years, beginning with the Upanishads in the sixth century B.C. They developed the concepts of the *Brahman*, absolute Being, the ultimate reality, of the *Atman*, the self, and of their fundamental unity. The *Bhagavad-Gita*, the most loved sacred book of the modern Hindu, introduced the concept of love of God for man and of man for God, expressed by the term *bhakti*, personal devotion. Every god in the Hindu pantheon has its own devotees. The *sutras* of the Hindu philosophers, the Upanishads and the *Bhagavad-Gita* constitute the triple foundation of Hinduism, which was developed between the eighth and fifteenth centuries into a variety of systems, which all still have their followers. Of these, Griffiths singles out three. The first is the *Advaita* school of Sankara (788–820 A.D.) which denied the reality of the external world in order to maintain the absolute purity and transcendence of the divine nature, and maintained that only the *Brahman* existed. The world was *maya*, illusion, and only *avidya*, ignorance, made it appear otherwise. The second is the school of Ramanuja (1017–1137), who regarded both the universe and the soul as modes of God's existence. The third, that of Madhva (1198–1278) taught a dualism (*Dvaita*), holding that God, the world and souls were distinct, but all as equally eternal. What the *Vedanta* lacked was the concept of creation. With the concept *bhakti*, devotion, we have come a long way from the monistic pantheism of Sankara. But we need to remember that each distinct god remains a manifestation of the one absolute Being, the *Brahman*.

This is apparent in the practice of yoga in all its different forms. With its discipline of posture, breathing and the control of the senses and the mind, the system of yoga is intended to bring the heart and the mind into a state in which it can be absolutely one with God, the ultimate reality, and participate in the divine consciousness. In *Return to the Centre*, Griffiths describes the various schools of yoga in some detail. According to his biographer, he was himself a practitioner, conceiving it to be a method of integration by which all the faculties of the soul were drawn into the inner centre and gathered into union with the divine Spirit, experiencing liberation, *moksha*, even in this life. *Purusha*, the spirit or consciousness, was separated from its attachment to nature and matter, *prakriti*, to realize in isolation, *kaivalya*, its pure spirituality. Thus yoga is the epitome of Hinduism, the aim of which, in the words of R. C. Zaehner, is 'to achieve the highest bliss in which personality is lost in that which both underlies and transcends it'. In yoga and therefore Hinduism, liberation and union with the divine is thus achieved by techniques of self-discipline without a redeemer. Hinduism has no Creator God, and no God who became man for the sake of our redemption.

Since Hinduism lacks a transcendent Creator, it may legitimately be asked whether it has any truly transcendent dimension. Griffiths defines transcendence as 'the power to give oneself totally to another, to transcend one's self in surrendering to the higher Self, the *Atman*, the spirit within'.[57] But is surrendering one's self to one's higher Self a giving of oneself totally to another? In Hindu terms it is a self-giving, because the *Atman* is also the 'infinite, transcendent holy Mystery which is what is signified by "God" or "Heaven"', which is 'also present in the world', and 'has its kingdom, its reign, its dwelling among men'.[58] Transcendence in this sense, he tells us, is to be found in the sacred books of all religions. Having in Hindu fashion internalized transcendence, he now seeks to externalize it by identifying it with a God who is not only present in the self but in the world and heaven. So he can speciously go on to insist that in Christian mysticism the human is not, as in Hinduism, absorbed in the divine, but while sharing in the divine nature, knowledge and bliss, it remains distinct in itself. This claim is often made and Christian mystics have multifarious experiences which they describe in a multitude of ways. Nevertheless throughout the whole of the mystic literature in the Christian tradition, there runs the theme of experiences of a complete, if only fleeting, unification with God in which all sense of personal identity is lost. According to his biographer, Griffiths enjoyed mystical experiences while reading the Hindu and Buddhist scriptures. He says nothing about whether these differed from any specifically Christian mystical experiences which may have come his way. He endorses the statement of the 14th century mystic Eckhart, 'Man and animal in God are God.' For Griffiths, the knowledge of the self in its ultimate ground is identical with a knowledge of God. This is Hinduism, not Christianity, and Griffiths knows it. In the doctrine of *advaita* man knows with the non-dual knowledge of God because he is identical with God. In Christianity, Griffiths claims man knows himself in identity with God (a view surely coloured by his Hinduism), but remains distinct from him. Hinduism and

Christianity are in contrast, but have a profound affinity. Griffiths believes they will ultimately converge.

We have surely the right to speak of a common tradition among the different religious traditions . . . witnessing to a common origin and a common goal. As the different religions draw nearer to one another in mutual respect, seeking the ultimate truth to which they all alike bear witness, may we not hope that they may eventually arrive at unity?[59]

In Griffiths, the convergence is already taking place. Whatever Christian doctrine he touches upon he sees through Hindu eyes. Thus repentance for him is not the biblical repentance toward God (*Acts 20:21*), involving a new mind and a change of direction, but in accordance with all we have found in him so far, a turning within, a return to the source and origin to be found in the inner self.[60]

He similarly transforms the doctrine of the incarnation until it is pure Hinduism. He concedes that the incarnation provides Christianity with a basis in history which Hinduism lacks: God became man at a certain time and in a certain place. But he undermines the importance of such an event, indeed of any event, by telling us that history has only significance when it is mythical, a symbol of universal significance. The incarnation is only a sign, and though it makes the mystery of ultimate reality present, it does not fully disclose it. For Griffiths it has no finality: for him, therefore, the statement of John 1:18 ('No man hath seen God at any time; the only begotten son, which is in the bosom of the Father, he hath declared him') cannot hold good. The uniqueness of Christ as a revelation of God is on the same level as the uniqueness of Buddha and Krishna as revealers of God.[61] That is, it is a uniqueness which is not unique. This must be the case if Hinduism is true, and only if Hinduism is true, for in Hinduism every man is an incarnation, a manifestation of the divine because the soul of man, the *Atman*, is one with the *Brahman*, the ultimate, the transcendent mystery. There is a hidden presence of Christ in every man[62] and one self incarnate in humanity.[63] Christ is the true *Atman* of every man. Griffiths may have set out with the intention of making Christianity more acceptable to Hinduism; he has ended by Hinduizing Christianity.

It is possible that he would not regard this verdict as a reproach, but rather a sign of ignorance on the part of the one who voiced it. For to Griffiths, as for the pluralists, all religions are limited, because historically conditioned and in a state of evolution, and no single religion contains the whole truth. He would agree with Dr Runcie that to know only one religion is to know none:

it is not possible to confine the Spirit to one scripture alone. We have to learn to recognize the voice of the Spirit in every scripture and discover the hidden source from which all scriptures come.[64]

This is so because behind each limited religion, which is necessarily corrupt through its historical conditioning, lies a cosmic covenant, a universal revelation given to all mankind through nature and the soul.[65] This predates the covenant with Moses and the special revelation to the Jews. It points to a religion in which man knows himself as a part of nature, having kinship with the earth and sky; with the plants, animals and birds and also having communion with the spirits of the dead:

In the depths of the subconscious we are at one with all nature and all humanity, open to the divine spirit which is in all, not enclosed in a separate identity in an alien world.[66]

This cosmic revelation lies at the heart of the tradition of the East, and needs to be recovered. A return to biblical Christianity would be to return to the mistake of the Reformation and lead to an impasse.[67] What is needed is a meeting in fertile union of the masculine mind of the West and the feminine mind of the East.[68]

Three particular aspects of Griffiths' teaching require special comment. The first is his interpretation of the sexual images prevalent in Hinduism. During his early days in India, he sat beside a shrine on a river bank, which contained a roughly carved *lingam* and *yoni*, images of the male and female genitalia. In them he found yet one more expression of the sacred, of faith in their regenerative powers and an awareness of the holiness of nature. In the central shrine of every Hindu temple there may be only a *lingam*, which he explains as representing the formless divinity, the absolute godhead which is beyond all name and form. The *lingam*, a natural symbol of the source of life, was to the metaphysical sense of ancient India no mere biological reality, but indicative of the Absolute Being, which is life, consciousness and bliss, saccidananda. A less naïve mind would see in this symbolism not perhaps the deification of sex but certainly a turning away from the Creator, who alone is blessed for ever (*Rom. 1:25*), to a worship of the creature. Hinduism is here far removed from the Bible attitude which regards sex as part of the created order, to be received from the Creator with thanksgiving, but nowhere suggests the sex organs as a starting-point for the worship of God. Griffiths, however, sees the fertility cults of primitive religions, which God calls an abomination, as pointers to the universal presence of the sacred.[69] The robust words of Bonhoeffer seem an adequate comment: 'To long for the transcendent when you are in your wife's arms is, to put it mildly, a lack of taste, and it is certainly not what God expects of us'.[70]

Secondly, Griffiths seems to accept the Hindu distinction between the gross and subtle senses, and between gross and subtle matter. The subtle senses are present in all men, but generally underdeveloped. They belong to a psychic world lying between the physical and spiritual worlds. It was not in virtue of his divinity that Christ performed his miracles, but through the psychic powers latent in all men. But the *kenosis*, the self-emptying, of Christ in his incarnation did not involve him stripping himself of any of his divine attributes. Griffiths states that the psychic powers, known as *siddhis*, can be developed to a high degree by the practice of *yoga*. He has no difficulty in accepting the materializations affected by Sai Baba, a guru who has many devotees in the West, or the process by which the Shiva *lingam* grows within the body of Swami Premananda to issue from his mouth as a small statue. On one occasion Swami Premananda visited Saccidananda Ashram and, sitting beside Griffiths, produced out of nowhere sandalwood powder, which he poured into Griffiths' hand. Such manifestations of the supernatural, which are real enough, are not to be explained by reference to the parapsychological. They are the result of demonic activity, and indicative of a demonic element at the heart of Hinduism. The preternatural physical and mental torment endured by John Lennon, who recited the Hindu Om, in the closing months of his life, can be explained only by the phenomenon of demon possession. Here we are touching what R. C. Zaehner has called the dark side of Hinduism, which is entirely ignored by our pluralists. This has been most recently demonstrated, according to a report in the March 1995 issue of *The Evangelical Times*, by the killing of two girls and a boy as a sacrifice to the goddess Meladi in her temple at Surenra.

Thirdly, Griffiths has an idiosyncratic view of the cross, which he sees as the convergence of two opposite movements, man's ascent to God, and the descent of God into this world. The former is man's effort to transcend the barriers of space and to reach the infinite transcendence. The latter is the incarnation, which is more than God taking on human flesh in the person of Christ, for it is also the Spirit's communication of himself to matter since the moment of creation. God came down in response to man's reaching out to him. The ascent of man to God represents the whole trend of oriental thought.[71] All this runs completely counter to biblical teaching:

Let this mind be in you, which was also in Christ Jesus, who, being in the form of God, thought it not robbery to be equal with God: but made himself of no reputation, and took upon him the form of a servant, and was make in the likeness of men: and being found in fashion as a man, he humbled himself and became obedient unto death, even the death of the cross (*Phil. 2:5–8*).

The influence of Griffiths on the inter-faith movement is second only to that of Thomas Merton, whom we are about to consider. Griffiths' ashram received a constant stream of visitors from all over the world. He was a regular participant in inter-faith gatherings in India and in his world-wide travels was in continual demand as a lecturer and director of seminars and retreats. The impact he made thus strengthened that of his writings. Griffiths' synthesis of Christianity and Hinduism was paralleled by Thomas Merton's identification of Christianity and Buddhism, at least in its mystical aspects. Born in 1915, Merton was educated at an English school and at Cambridge before entering Columbia University in 1935. A strong reaction against Western technology and consumerism led him to a brief flirtation with communism and an equally short period of hedonism. His interest in Eastern religions was stimulated by Aldous Huxley's

Ends and Means, a comparison of leading mediaeval Catholic mystics with the Buddha and the Hindu Sankara. An encounter with an Indian yogi, Dr Mahanambrata Brahmachari, who encouraged him to read the life of St. Francis, St. Augustine's *Confessions* and Thomas à Kempis' *Imitation of Christ*, paradoxically convinced him that the West, after all, had the answers to ultimate questions for which he was seeking. He became a Roman Catholic in 1938, and three years later entered the Trappist monastery of Gethsemani, Kentucky. He was ordained priest in 1949. His systematic study of Eastern religions dated from that time, a study in which he was helped by Dr D. T. Suzuki, the leading exponent of Zen Buddhism in the West, and by Dr John C. Wu, an orientalist and convert to Catholicism. His chief writings are *The Way of Chang Tzu* (1965), *Mystics and the Zen Masters* (1967), *Zen and the Birds of Appetite* (1968) and the posthumous *Asian Journal of Thomas Merton* (1973, English edition, 1974). The last title is a record of a journey which took him through the length and breadth of India, to Sri Lanka and Bangkok. It was a personal exploration of the East long wished for and long postponed, and it also gave him the opportunity to acquire a first-hand knowledge of Tibetan monasticism while fulfilling his official duty of inspecting Catholic monastic houses. The journal is not only a travelogue, but a record of the extensive study of Buddhism and Hinduism which he continued as he journeyed, and also of his encounters with the Dalai Lama and other important representatives of Eastern spirituality.

Chang Tzu (396–286 B.C.) was an adherent of Taoism founded by the mythical Lao Tzu. Tao is the eternal, nameless, ultimate reality, transcending all concepts and all modes of visualization. It embodied perfection, a perfection not to be aimed at by a necessarily self-defeating conscious pursuit, but by the practice of *Wu-Wei*, which Merton translated 'non-ado'. In using this technique, we would be acting without effort in harmony with the hidden power that drives the universe. If we set aside all egoistic craving, we would become perfect instruments for the Tao to act through us. By thus losing ourselves, we would find ourselves in our true identity. To Merton this constituted an equivalent of the gospel teaching that by losing our life we would save it. His mentor Dr Wu identified the Tao with the Word of St. John's Gospel, who was with God from the beginning, and was God. Merton accepted this interpretation. It was his fixed conviction that the way to re-Christianize the West was through the East, where contemplation has always been practised and held in high regard.

Chang Tzu developed the teaching of Lao Tzu through his dialectical belief in the complementarity of opposites. This precluded the acceptance of any absolute. If a limited and conditioned good was taken as an absolute it would become an evil, because of the consequent exclusion of the complementary element it needed to be fully good. Like Lao Tzu, he believed the effort to be virtuous would prevent our attainment of virtue, which must always be the outcome of our spontaneous action, expressing our very nature. Chang Tzu advocated 'the fasting of the heart'; we are to ignore our understanding and follow our spirit, our whole being. If we empty ourselves of our faculties, we will arrive at inner unity and our heart will be full of light. He thus recommended the passivity which is the teaching of so many mystics, but against which others warn us. Merton found in Chang Tzu's approach an affinity with Christ's emphasis on poverty of spirit.

The spiritual heirs of Chang Tzu were the Chinese Buddhists of the seventh to the tenth centuries A.D., who were not concerned with words and formulae about reality, but with grasping it directly and existentially. Such a grasp was Merton's consuming passion, and led him naturally from Taoism to Zen Buddhism. The heart of Zen Buddhism is expressed in a quotation in his *Asian Journal*, which he took from another book by a fellow Catholic monk who had anticipated him in his passion for Eastern religion, Dom Aelred Graham's *Conversations: Christian and Buddhist*. In Zen the

realizer does not stand outside reality but may be said to be at least part of that reality, a self-manifestation of reality as such.

Self-realization, self-fulfilment and liberation are achieved when one discovers oneself as this self-manifestation of reality.[72] The Tao, ultimate reality, is within. Thus in Taoism and Zen, as in Hinduism, man is divine. In fact, it is difficult to distinguish between Zen and its parent Buddhism, and Merton often uses the terms interchangeably. A possible differentiation may be drawn from the fact that in Zen enlightenment is held to occur instantaneously, while in Buddhism the concept of gradual enlightenment is more usual. But instantaneous enlightenment is also found in Mahayana Buddhism. The latter developed out of Madhyamika, the so-called middle path of Buddhism, based on the teachings of Nagarjuna in the second or third century B.C. It sought by a dialectical process to reach a position above reason, thus delivering the human mind from entanglement and passion and bringing it into true freedom. During his Asian journey, Merton studied Madhyamika deeply. Historically it was the origin of Zen Buddhism. Its process of criticism led to *sunyata*, the utter negation of thought as revelatory of the real. The death of thought resulted in the birth of *prajna*, knowledge devoid of distinction, the direct intuition of the unconditional. The basic tenet of Madhyamika is that the absolute, transcending thought, is thoroughly immanent in experience.[73] Zen, with the dual technique of meditation while sitting upright with the legs in the crossed position, and the posing of *koans*, logically insoluble riddles, similarly aimed at transcending the intellect and evoking pure intuition, thus catapulting the disciple into direct confrontation with reality. Both Madhyamika and Zen clearly descended immediately from the teaching of the Buddha himself, who is recorded as saying,

To hold that the world is eternal or to hold that it is not, or to agree to any other of the propositions you adduce, Vaccha, is the jungle of theorizing, attended by ill, distress, perturbation and fever; it conduces not to detachment, passionless tranquillity, to knowledge and wisdom of Nirvana. This is the danger I perceive in these views, which makes me discard them all.[74]

So Murti, the authority on Madhyamika, whom Merton frequently quotes, could rightly comment:

The rejection of theories (*ditthi*) is itself the means by which the Buddha is led to the non-conceptual knowledge of the absolute, and not vice versa.[75]

Merton corresponded with his mentor in Zen, D. T. Suzuki, since the late 1950s, and met him in 1964, when he participated in the tea ceremony with him. Merton approached the ceremony with reverence and attention, but Suzuki treated it in a perfunctory fashion, thus emphasizing its point: ordinary functions, like eating and drinking, could be used to reveal the underlying mystery of all things, their transcendent aspect and eternal dimension. In this way, it spoke to Merton of the Eucharist: those who shared in it experienced a spirit of communion. It could induce *Nirvana*, enlightenment, purity of heart, or in Christian terms 'life in the Spirit', interchangable terms for the indescribable experience of intuited reality, which frees one from delusions, including ego consciousness. It brought about harmony with everything, so that life could be experienced as it really was, fulfilling the need for transcendence and ultimate meaning.

But the seeing of Zen, beyond conceptualization, was in essence a non-seeing. Merton regarded it as analogous to the apophatic way of the earliest Christian monks, the Desert Fathers, and of some of the later Christian mystics, the way, that is, of denial: God was to be known through what he was not, not through what he was. Merton believed that the Zen masters had enjoyed supernatural experiences akin to those of the Christian mystics. In the earlier stages of this thought, however, he stressed the difference between the two. In Zen and Buddhism generally, the obstacle to enlightenment and the abandonment of the egocentric view was *avidya*, ignorance, for which man was not responsible. In Christianity, it was original sin and the fall of man which led him to manipulate the world in defiance of God and his laws. Buddhism endeavoured to cope with man's condition by advocating right mindfulness: through meditation man became aware that he did not possess a separate self, and gradually or suddenly entered the state of *Nirvana*, which Merton defined as perfect awareness and perfect compassion, 'the wide openness of Being itself, the realization that Pure Being is Infinite Giving, or that Absolute Emptiness is Absolute Compassion'.[76] He contended that Zen meditation shattered the false self and restored us to the state of paradisal innocence which preceded the fall. But he allowed himself to be persuaded by

Suzuki that paradise had never been lost, and therefore did not need to be regained.[77] He knew that the Buddhist regarded the attainment of *Nirvana* as a transformation of consciousness in which grace as Christians understood it played no part. Yet he argued, 'One can hardly help feeling that the illumination of the genuine Zen experience seems to open out into an unconscious demand for grace – a demand that is perhaps answered without being understood,' and queried, 'Is it perhaps already grace?'[78] In his *Asian Journal* he quoted another author who had pondered over the same problem, and concluded that grace was certainly to be found in Buddhism, by a claim that 'grace' was a portmanteau word:

The word grace corresponds to a whole dimension of spiritual experience; it is unthinkable that this should be absent from one of the great religions of the world.[79]

It is the function of grace to condition man's homecoming to the centre; grace is the attraction of the centre itself 'which provides the incentive to start on the Way and the energy to face and overcome its many and various obstacles. Likewise grace is the welcoming hand into the centre when man finds himself at long last on the brink of the great divide where all familiar landmarks have disappeared'.[80] Here grace is entirely divorced from biblical grace, 'the grace of God which is given you by Jesus Christ' (*1 Cor. 1:4*). Grace in the Bible is never an abstract concept, and never divorced from the person of Jesus. Merton's last word on the relationship of *avidya* and original sin was virtually to identify them.

Both Christianity and Buddhism agree that the root of man's problems is that his consciousness is all fouled up and he does not apprehend reality as it fully and really is; that the moment he looks at something he begins to interpret it in ways that are prejudiced and predetermined to fit a certain wrong picture of the world, in which he exists as an individual ego in the centre of things. This is called by Buddhism avidya, or ignorance . . . Christianity says almost the same things in terms of original sin.[81]

Ultimately he came to regard the theological comparison of Buddhism and Christianity as a blind alley; 'to what extent does the theology of a theologian without experience claim to interpret correctly the "experienced theology" of the mystic who is perhaps not able to articulate the meaning of his experience in a satisfactory way?'[82] For Merton, Christianity and Buddhism 'in their original purity point beyond all divisions between this and that'.[83] This must necessarily involve the abolition of the distinction between the Creator and the creature, which to the Christian is fundamental. It is not surprising, after all we have discovered, to find Merton declaring in an unpublished letter, 'I am as much a Chinese Buddhist by temperament and spirit as I am a Christian'.[84]

In his attempt to find affinities between Christianity and Buddhism Merton appealed to the fourteenth-century Flemish mystic Eckhart, on whom Griffiths had similarly relied for his assimilation of Hinduism to Christianity. In Eckhart he found a delineation of an inner awareness of God corresponding to the intuition in Zen of limitless inner freedom. He quotes Eckhart's sermon 28: 'A man should be so poor that he is not and has not a place for God to act in. To reserve a place would be to maintain distinctions.'[85] He interprets Eckhart's 'utmost poverty' as nothingness, the elimination of the ego equivalent to *sunyata*, which enabled man to be filled with God. If we imagine we empty ourselves to make room for God we are still under the delusion we have a separate ego. All concepts of God and self must vanish, until only 'pure being' remains. In conformation, he cites a passage from Eckhart's sermon 23 in the same vein: 'There is something in the soul so closely akin to God that it is already one with Him and needs never be united with Him'.[86] In true poverty, when the false ego has died, our true nature emerges and manifests the living presence of God within us. All this seemed to Merton akin to Zen, and to 'the discovery not that one sees Buddha but that one *is* Buddha',[87] without any image of Buddha to see, but only 'a Void in which no image was even conceivable'.[88] This may be Buddhism, but it is a far cry from the Christian experience of being a new creature in Christ Jesus (*2 Cor. 5:17*).

Other aspects of Buddhism appealed to Merton. He studied the mandala, a circular representation of the universe, containing images symbolic of the cosmic nature of the Buddha, and used as an object of meditation with the aim of becoming the Buddha enthroned in one's own centre. The mandala takes us back to mysticism. According to the leading authority on the mandala quoted by Merton its use shows the meditator that the principle of salvation lies within him: the images he sees come from his own heart, deifying him and replacing his soul's agitation by a steady serene light.[89] It is consistent with this view of salvation that he has earlier quoted, without any apparent demur, a classic Sufi saying, 'To say that I am God is not pride, it is perfect modesty'.[90]

Merton's attention was also drawn to Tantrism. The Tantras were a body of esoteric Hindu literature which emphasized the worship of the female essence of the universe, the Divine Mother or *Shakti*. Tantric thought was introduced into Buddhism by the Tibetan king Trisong-Detsan who reigned in the eighth century. The meditation it practised placed heavy emphasis on symbolic rites, gestures, postures and the use of secret formulae. At one stage Merton considered Tantric initiation. As with the mandala, its aim was to set free the divine light present in each one of us, although enveloped in a web of our own weaving.

During his time in Asia Merton had three meetings with the Dalai Lama, whom he found to be a man of high 'attainment'.[91] He does not give many details of that conversation but he does tell us that they concentrated on meditation and the difference between Christian and Tibetan monasticism. In their second encounter they discussed how meditation could start with an object, an image or a name. In northern India, Merton met many Tibetan monks, the most notable of whom was Chatral Rimpoche, who at Ghoom near Darjeeling had meditated in seclusion for thirty years. Merton's conversation with him focused on *dzogchen*, the ultimate perfect emptiness beyond God. Afterwards he commented:

The unspoken or half-spoken message of the talk was our complete understanding of each other as people who were somehow *on the edge* of a great realization and knew it, and were trying, somehow or other, to go out and get lost in it – and that it was a grace for us to meet one another.[92]

Yet the climax of Merton's journey came not with his meetings with individuals, however impressive he found them, but with his visits to the ruined temple cities of Mahabalipuram, south of Madras, and Polonnaruwa in Sri Lanka, with their massive statues of the Buddha:

The silence of the extraordinary faces. The great smiles. Huge and yet subtle. Filled with every possibility, questioning nothing, knowing everything, rejecting nothing, the peace not of emotional resignation but of Madhyamika, of sunyata, that has seen through every question without trying to discredit anyone or anything – without establishing some other argument . . .

Looking at these figures I was suddenly, almost forcibly jerked clean out of the habitual, half-tied vision of things, and an inner clearness, clarity, as if exploding from the rocks themselves, became evident and obvious . . . The thing about this is that there is no puzzle, no problem, and really no 'mystery'. All problems are resolved and everything is clear, simply because what matters is clear. The rock, all matter, all life is charged with dharmakayea [i.e., the cosmic body of the Buddha, the essence of all beings] . . . everything is emptiness and everything is compassion. I don't know when in my life I have had such a sense of beauty and spiritual validity running together in one aesthetic illumination. Surely, with Mahabalipuram and Polonnaruwa my Asian pilgrimage has come clear and purified itself. I mean, I know and have seen what I was obscurely looking for. I don't know what else remains but I have now seen and have pierced through the surface and have got beyond the shadow and disguise.[93]

What remains for a Christian is Christ and the reconciliation with God he effected for us on his cross (*2 Cor. 5:19*). Merton's transport before the relics of Buddhism leaves that out of account. In contrast, we can turn to John Stott, that champion of the uniqueness of Christ in an increasingly apostate age:

I have entered many Buddhist temples . . . and stood respectfully before the statue of the Buddha, his legs crossed, arms folded, a remote look on his face, detached from the agonies of the world. But each time after a while I have had to turn away. And in imagination I have turned instead to that lonely, twisted, tortured figure on the cross, nails through hands and feet, back lacerated, limbs wrenched, brow bleeding from thorn pricks, mouth dry and intolerably thirsty, plunged in God-forsaken darkness. That is the God for me! He laid aside his immunity to pain. He entered our world of flesh and blood, tears and death. He suffered for us. Our sufferings become more manageable in the light of his.[94]

Although he thus owed his deepest mystical experience to Buddhism, Merton had a great appreciation for Hinduism, without studying it with the intensity he devoted to Zen Buddhism. In 1967, in a work published after his death, *Opening the Bible*, he explained that he preferred Zen as a non-speculative and non-systematic way to obtain a direct vision of the ground of being, in contrast to the deeply speculative nature of Hinduism. Nevertheless, he considered the Upanishads 'the most profound contemplative collection of texts ever written dealing with the metaphysical unity of Being and with the yogic consciousness of that unity in concentration and in self-transcending wisdom.'[95]

In the 1960s Merton studied seriously a classic manual on Yoga, *The Yoga Aphorisms of Pantanjali*, taking extensive notes on the eight steps it outlines for the stilling of the mind (abstention from evil, the various observances, posture, control of vital energy, the withdrawal of the senses or interiorization, concentration, meditation and union), which were intended to lead to a state of pure consciousness devoid of desire and without any subject-object distinction. Here he again found similarities with the Desert Fathers and also with St. John of the Cross. He was especially impressed with Ramana Maharshi (1879–1950), whom he regarded as a modern Desert Father. Ramana Maharshi relentlessly asked the question 'Who am I?', and so was led to eliminate the temporary and superficial ego to arrive at the true self, which he defined in the formula we are already familiar with, Sat-Cit-Ananda, the Absolute or Ultimate Reality. Merton's own contemplative experience had led him to the same goal, from the thought that 'I am this' to the pure consciousness 'I am', a pure monism incompatible with Christian theism. But Merton did not recognize the incompatibility. He was acquainted with the writings of Monanchin and Le Saux, the mentors of Dom Bede Griffiths. The latter had argued that *advaita*, Hindu monism, had its counterpart in Christianity, appealing for support to John 17: 21, 'That they all may be one, as thou, Father art in me, and I in thee, that they also may be one in us'. In an unpublished letter, Merton declared that a Hindu *sadhu*, or holy man, could love and know God better than a Christian and therefore be closer to him.[96] God, he argued, was not bound by any theological framework, and the Holy Spirit might manifest himself more strongly in a Hindu than in a Christian monk such as himself. Although he was aware that in *Isvara*, Hinduism had a concept of a personal God, he was more attracted to its prevalent monism. His *Asian Journal* is studded with quotations from Sankara's *Crest-Jewel of Discrimination*, all stressing the need to rise above name and form and to realize that only One exists, and 'That is Thou'.

Griffiths retained an interest in the conversion of Hindus, and tried to convert them by showing them how much in their religion was intrinsically Christian. Thomas Merton had no concern for the conversion of either Hindu or Buddhist. In the preface to a new translation of the *Bhagavad-Gita*, he wrote,

It is in surrendering a false and illusory liberty on the personal level that man unites himself with the inner ground of reality and freedom in himself which is the will of God, of Krishna, of Providence, of Tao. These concepts do not all exactly coincide, but they have much in common. It is by remaining open to an infinite number of unexpected possibilities which transcend his own imagination and capacity to plan that man really fulfils his own need for freedom. The *Gita*, like the Gospels, teaches us to live in awareness of an inner truth that exceeds the grasp of our thought and cannot be subject to our control.[97]

Christianity and Eastern religions could be mutually enriching and might ultimately converge:

I believe that by openness to Buddhism, to Hinduism, and these great Asian traditions, we stand a wonderful chance of learning more about the potentiality of our own traditions, because they have gone, from the natural point of view, so much deeper into this than we have. The combination of the natural techniques and the graces of the other things that have been manifested in Asia and the Christian liberty of the gospel should bring us all at last to that full and transcendent liberty which is beyond mere cultural differences and mere externals – and mere this and that.[98]

In the last analysis, however, there is no need for convergence; we are already one. During his journey Merton spoke in Calcutta at the first World Summit Conference organized by the Temple of Understanding, which we met in our first chapter. There he expressed his underlying belief:

We discover an older unity. My dear brothers, we are already one. But we imagine that we are not. And what we have to recover is our original unity. What we have to be is what we are.[99]

Unlike Merton, Griffiths does not explicitly refer to apophatic theology, the way of negation, based on the belief that God cannot be known by his attributes, but only by denying all that he is not. He did, however, appeal to Dionysius the Areopagite, the fifth-century Syrian monk through whose writings it entered both Latin and Orthodox Christianity. Apophatic theology has always been closely associated with mysticism; one of Dionysius' most important works was *Mystical Theology*. In her classic study of mysticism, Evelyn Underhill traced a line of apophatic mystics running from Dionysius to Eckhart and beyond. We have met Eckhart as a mentor of both Griffiths and Merton. Behind Dionysius, however, lies the Neoplatonist Plotinus (205–270 A.D.) and his ineffable One whom he knew only in moments of ecstatic union. Griffiths argues that the religious wisdom of the East entered Catholicism at this early date, because Plotinus' thought was transmitted to Western and Eastern Christendom alike. Certainly the Hellenistic world was in contact with the East, and whatever sources other than Plato influenced Plotinus, Plotinus exercised a dominant influence on the thought of Dionysius. In his Younghusband Memorial Lecture, Dr Runcie also drew our attention to the negative way of the apophatic method and its importance in the different religious traditions. The apophatic way has a natural appeal for those who wish to bring the religions of the world together, for if God cannot be known in what he is, any god may be God. Although attempts have been made to give it a biblical base, it remains alien to the Bible, which continually brings before us the manifold attributes of God. Certainly it points us to the mystery of God; the finite mind of the creature cannot know the infinite Creator comprehensively, but what it can know of him through his self-revelation in creation, Scriptures and Christ, it can know clearly and, as the Reformers expressed it, perspicaciously: 'That which may be known of God is manifested in [men]; for God hath shewed it unto them. For the invisible things of him from the creation of the world are clearly seen, being understood by the things that are made, even his eternal power and Godhead' (*Rom. 1:19–20*).

Merton has been even more influential and acquired an even higher reputation for spirituality than Griffiths; his writings chime in with the syncretistic cast of modern thinking even more resonantly. We do well therefore to pay serious attention to the judgement to which extra importance accrues because it comes from within the Orthodox tradition in which apophatic theology is even more deeply embedded than in Latin Christianity:

Thomas Merton . . . constitutes a special threat to Christians because he presents himself as a contemplative Christian monk, and his work has already affected the vitals of Roman Catholicism, its monasticism . . . Father Merton wrote an appreciative introduction to a new translation of the 'Bhagavad Gita' . . . the spiritual manual or 'Bible' of all Hindus . . . [which] opposes almost every important teaching of Christianity. His book on the 'Zen Masters' . . . is based on a treacherous mistake: the assumption that all so-called 'mystical experiences' in every religion are true. He should have known better. The warnings against this are loud and clear, both in Holy Scripture and in the Holy Fathers.[100]

The thought of Griffiths and Merton ought also to be viewed in the light of the fact that their view that the Eastern religions with their inwardness have a claim to the spiritual leadership of the West is shared by one of the most implacable opponents of Christianity since the inter-faith movement sprang into life at the end of the nineteenth century. In 1875, Madame Helena P. Blavatsky founded the Theosophical Society. She wrote in her scrapbook for that year,

The Christians and scientists must be made to respect their Indian betters. The wisdom of India, her philosophy and achievement must be made known in Europe and America and the English be made to respect the natives of India and Tibet more than they do.[101]

Believing with Hinduism and Buddhism that the redemption of the individual, conceived as the attainment of oneness with ultimate reality, required a prolonged cycle of birth and rebirth through many reincarnations, Blavatsky asserted:

It is owing to this law of spiritual development that mankind will become freed from its false gods and find itself finally – SELF-REDEEMED.[102]

Blavatsky claimed to write in telepathic communication with the 'Masters' of the ancient wisdom who directed her, ignoring the fact that supernatural guidance which is not from God is demonic in origin. In a brochure, the Theosophical Society made its anti-Christian stance explicit: its aim was to 'oppose . . . every form of dogmatic theology, especially the Christian, which the chiefs of the Society regarded as particularly pernicious'. The gods of all the monotheistic religions, made by man in his own likeness, were 'a blasphemous and sorry caricature of the ever knowable'.[103] Ultimately all religions must merge:

Esoteric Philosophy reconciles all nations, strips every one of its outward human garments, and shows the root of each to be identical with that of every other religion.[104]

Madame Blavatsky agrees with Merton; we are to become one, which we already are. Significantly, the Theosophical Society for many years called one of its publications *Lucifer*. In its Spring issue, 1956, *The Voice*, a syncretist magazine published originally in Lewes, Sussex, and now in South Africa, described Madame Blavatsky's writings as the ultimate authority for occultists everywhere. One wonders if the direction of Griffiths' life was in any way determined by the theosophical writings read to him in his youth by his mother's friend. Dom Bede Griffiths, Father Thomas Merton and Madame Blavatsky constitute an unholy alliance. Griffiths moved Christ and Christianity from the centre to the margin, Merton relegated them to the periphery, Madame Blavatsky wished to eliminate them altogether. The progession is logical and inevitable.

CHAPTER III

The Churches and Inter-Faith

1 : *The Roman Catholic Church*

The work of Griffiths anticipated the transformation of the attitude of the Roman Catholic Church to other religions at the Second Vatican Council (1962–1965), while that of Merton was contemporaneous with it. The Council is another major landmark in the history of the inter-faith movement. Its first declaration, *Lumen Gentium*, holds out the hope of salvation to the adherents of all faiths and to those who seek God apart from Christ:

> The plan of salvation also includes those who acknowledge the Creator. In the first place among these are the Moslems, who, professing to hold the faith of Abraham, along with us adore the one merciful God, who on the last day will judge mankind. Nor is God himself far distant from those who in shadows and images seek the unknown God . . .
>
> Those also can attain to everlasting salvation who through no fault of their own do not know the gospel of Christ or His Church, yet sincerely worship God, and, moved by grace, strive to do His will as it is known to them through the dictates of conscience . . . Whatever goodness or truth is found among them is looked upon by the Church as a preparation for the gospel. She regards such qualities as given by Him Who enlightens all so that they may finally have life.[1]

The statement repeats the assertion of the pluralists that idolaters do not worship images, but the transcendent through images. Its concluding claim is a clear reference to John 1:9: 'That was the true Light, which lighteth every man that cometh into the world'. This interpretation of the verse is based on the view that John uses the term 'word' in the prologue to his gospel in its Platonic and Stoic sense. But such exegesis is erroneous. In his magisterial commentary on St. John's Gospel (S.P.C.K., London, 1955), C. K. Barrett demonstrates that John does not understand the term in this way, which would indeed point to the belief in a natural illumination of all men everywhere. The next verse, 'He was in the world, and the world was made by him, and the world knew him not', specifically precludes such an illumination.[2] Barrett shows that John's use of the *logos* concept was determined by the twofold Old Testament understanding of 'word' and 'wisdom'.[3] He goes on to show that the word 'light' in the Gospel is inseparable from the concept of judgement: the light shines upon every man for judgement, to reveal what he is.[4] John 1:9 is to be understood in the light of John 3:19: 'And this is the condemnation, that light is come into the world, and men loved darkness rather than light, because their deeds were evil'. The Council's declaration on the relationship of the Church to the non-Christian religions, *Nostra Aetate* contains the same faulty exegesis:

> Other religions . . . strive variously to answer the restless strivings of the human heart by proposing 'ways', which consist of teachings, rules of life, and sacred ceremonies. The Catholic Church rejects nothing which is true and holy in these religions. She looks with sincere respect upon those ways of conduct and of life which . . . often reflect a ray of that *Truth which enlightens all men.*[5]

Here we may pause to query the appropriateness of applying the description 'holy' to the non-Christian religions. We can happily agree that they contain elements of goodness and truth and that their adherents are capable of self-denial, compassion and otherworldliness. But this does not constitute holiness. In the Bible the term has a special significance. Holiness is the very essence of God, and the term expresses the contrast between divinity and creatureliness, while in the Eastern religions, as we have seen, the Creator-creature distinction is blurred. In the Bible, a glimpse of the holiness of God brings a deep conviction of moral uncleanness (*Isa. 6*), while one prominent Hindu has declared that it is a sin to call man a sinner. Holiness in the Old Testament expresses the mystery of God (*Isa. 45:15*), and is inseparably bound up with the concepts of redemption and salvation (*Isa. 48:18–22*). Israel in herself is unholy, but in his mercy God is calling out a holy remnant: his holiness issues in a new creation. What he began in the Old Testament is continued in the New. Christians are not morally perfect, but this does not detract from the uniqueness of Christianity. The scriptures of other faiths have nothing to say about God's deliberate creation of a holy nation (*1 Pet. 2:9*).

Vatican II, then, makes a very positive assessment of other religions. *Nostra Aetate* lists what it regards as their contributions:

In Hinduism men contemplate the divine mystery and express it through an unspent fruitfulness of myths and through searching philosophical inquiry. They seek release from the anguish of our condition through ascetical practices or deep meditation or a loving, trusting flight toward God. Buddhism in its multiple forms acknowledges the radical insufficiency of this shifting world. It teaches a path by which men, in a devout and confident spirit, can either reach a state of absolute freedom or obtain supreme enlightenment by their own efforts or by higher assistance . . . Upon the Moslems, too, the Church looks with esteem. They adore one God, living and enduring, merciful and all powerful, Maker of earth and Speaker to men. They strive to submit wholeheatedly to His inscrutable decrees . . . Though they do not acknowledge Jesus as God, they revere Him as a prophet. They also honor Mary, His virgin mother, at times they call on her, too, with devotion.[6]

All this ignores the facts that the Hindu 'flight toward God', like the Buddhist search, is a turning within, and that the Muslim God, though one, is not the Christian God, because he is not the Father of our Lord Jesus Christ, neither is he a God with whom it is possible to have any fellowship.

The teaching of Vatican II is conveniently summarized in an encyclical of Pope Paul VI, *Evangelii Nuntiandi*:

The church respects and esteems those non-Christian religions because they are the living expression of the soul of vast groups of people. They carry within them the echo of thousands of years of searching for God, a quest which is incomplete but often made with great sincerity and righteousness of heart. They possess an impressive patrimony of deeply religious texts. They have taught generations of people how to pray. They are all impregnated with innumerable 'seeds of the word' and can constitute a true preparation for the Gospel, to quote a felicitous term used by the Second Vatican Council and borrowed from Eusebius of Caesarea.[7]

The assumption is that the God of all faiths is the same God, and that prayer is always the same phenomenon, which we have found not to be the case. There is also the same assumption of the divine illumination of all men everywhere. It is true that there is backing for this belief in some of the early Fathers of the church but they were sometimes too much influenced by the thought forms of the Hellenistic world in which they lived, and saw the New Testament through Greek rather than Jewish eyes. In the case of St. John's use of the term *logos*, as we have seen, they made a serious error which has had disastrous consequences ever since. They conceived of Christ as a universal enlightener, 'the cosmic Christ', as some have subsequently called him. It is impossible to overemphasize the fact that there is no cosmic Christ in this sense. If the world religions and consequently their adherents were truly impregnated with 'seeds of the word' there would be no need for men to be 'born again, not of corruptible seed, but of incorruptible, by the word of God which liveth and abideth for ever' (*1 Pet. 1:23*).

Others may have been as active in the inter-faith scene, but none has been more visible, because of the prominence of his position and of his world-wide travels, than the present Pope, John Paul II. Perhaps the best known event of his pontificate was the World Day of Prayer for Peace he organized at Assisi on 27 October, 1986. This was his response to the designation of that year by the United Nations as the year of peace. He announced his intention of organizing such a day in his homily at a mass he celebrated in the presence of representatives of other Christian denominations at St. Paul Outside the Wall on 25 January: he wanted to involve the entire world in a movement of prayer for peace surpassing national boundaries and including believers of all religions.[8] His proposal met with the immediate acceptance of a prominent Buddhist, Nikkyo Niwano, president of the six million strong Japanese Buddhist association, 'Rissho Kosei-Kai', and founder of the World Conference of Religions for Peace which had organized the gathering at Kyoto in 1970, who was the only non-Christian observer at the Second Vatican Council. He replied that the Pope's initiative 'fully corresponds to our intentions', and that for some time he had hoped that the Pope would co-operate with the progress of inter-religious dialogue for peace.[9] On 28 September 1986 John Paul II gave a talk further explaining what he had in mind: all believers in God knew that 'mutual acceptance in reciprocal respect and in solidarity' was part of their service to God and man.[10] Neither Vatican II nor John Paul II have suggested that the church should abandon its task of evangelism, but the logical conclusion of this statement is that it should do precisely that. In the Great Commission Christ commanded his followers to go into all the nations and make disciples (*Matt. 28:19*). Obviously, this must be done with respect and love. In our humanity we certainly should have solidarity with all human beings; Christ taught us that we are all neighbours. But there can be no acceptance of, or solidarity with, other faiths if we do not all worship the same God, which we do not. The assumption that we do, however, is at the heart of all inter-faith thinking. We found it in Younghusband, the pluralists, Hans Küng, in Vatican II and Pope John Paul II.

On 22 October, 1986, John Paul II held a general audience in St. Peter's Square to celebrate the eighth aniversary of the inauguration of his pontificate. In his address, while declaring that there was no salvation except in Christ, he repeated the statements of Vatican II that 'Christ is united in a certain way with everyone',[11] and that in every faith there are 'the seeds of the word' and 'rays of the one truth'. Among these, he included 'prayer, often accompanied by fasting, by other penances and by pilgrimages to sacred places held in veneration'. But the instinct to pray needs no seed of the Word; it is the result of man's retention, although in defaced fashion, of the image of God in which he was created. Penances and pilgrimages to sacred places, so far from being reflections of the 'rays of the one truth', are evidence of man's blindness to the truth, because they are always undertaken to acquire merit, while God declares that salvation is always a free gift which can never be earned: 'by grace ye are saved through faith; and that not of yourselves: it is the gift of God' (*Eph. 2:8*). John Paul II went on to explain what he intended to happen at Assisi. There would be no praying together, because common prayer between the different faiths was impossible, but their representatives would pray in each other's presence, thus manifesting their 'respect for the prayer of others and for the attitude of others before the Divinity'. The fact that Christians prayed apart while others prayed, also in their own appointed places and according to their own traditions, would itself by a 'humble and sincere witness to Christ, Lord of the Universe'. Such a being present to pray with other adorers of the living and true God would be of limitless value.[12] The suggestion is that Christian prayer would be more efficacious when the prayers of those of other faiths were added to it.

The Day of Prayer for Peace on 27 October, 1986 began, after an opening address by the Pope, with an ecumenical service of Christians in the Cathedral of San Rufino, while members of other faiths prayed simultaneously in their separate meeting-places. Dr Runcie and the Dalai Lama participated. In addition to Buddhists, Hindus, Sikhs, Muslims, Baha'is, and Shintoists, representatives of primitive cults including snake worshippers from Togo were among the gathering. The Pope's opening address emphasized its purpose: it was not an inter-religious conference, but a Day of Prayer for Peace. He did, however, stress that the very diversity of the religions taking part would express 'a relationship with a supreme power', which could achieve more for peace than men acting on their own. The faiths were to pray separately, but they would be praying to the same God.[13] Towards the end of the day, Christians met with non-Christians in the Basilica of St. Francis. Each faith was allowed five minutes to pray in the manner of its tradition, with intervals of silence between the prayers. Thus the Day of Prayer for Peace at Assisi was a time of inter-faith worship. It was remarkable in another way. Immediately before it, John Paul II appealed to the warring factions throughout the world to lay down their arms for its duration, a call which was heeded in Nicaragua, El Salvador and elsewhere. Its real significance, however, was religious. In a theological assessment of its importance, Jorge Mejia, the Vice-President of the Pontifical Commission *Iustitia et Pax* spoke of it as demonstrating the 'hidden convergence' or 'incipient but real unity' of the world religions which underlay their profound differences, differences which 'from God's point of view did not constitute an obstacle to their coming together for prayer, but on the contrary made it desirable'.[14] We are back with Sir Francis Younghusband's 'greater religion yet to be' and Thomas Merton's unity which we already have but need to recover.

The year 1986 showed Pope John Paul II very active on the inter-faith front. In the spring he paid a ten-day visit to India, beginning in New Delhi, where he had a dialogue with the Dalai Lama. The theme of the visit was 'The Call of the Lord to Unity'. In context this seems to imply unity among the world religions. In his meeting with the Dalai Lama he called for all religions to collaborate in the cause of humanity. In Madras, where he addressed a gathering of representatives of India's main religions, he went further. Although he similarly argued that the dialogue between religions should focus on the problems of human suffering and oppression, he also talked about the need to respect and be open to the convictions of others. The Indian press interpreted the Pope as stressing the unity of religions and in particular the Indianness of Christianity. This was a natural inference from John Paul's talk about the goodness to be found within India's ancient religion. In Madras he went to the extent of allowing his forehead to be marked with *vibhuti*, the sacred ash offered to idols, which must have seemed to Hindus an unqualified endorsement of their religion, and which can only be construed as at least a partial acceptance of the truth claims of Hinduism. In Bombay he told a mass youth rally to follow the teachings of their great sages of the past whose words contained perennial wisdom and truth.[15] The summer found the Pope in Seoul, where he extolled the virtues of Buddhism:

In the great ethical and religious visions of Buddhism, of Confucianism, the path to the renewal of self and to the consolidation of the whole people in virtue and in nobility of purpose, the profound reverence for life and nature, the quest for truth and harmony, the self-abnegation and compassion, the ceaseless striving to transcend – these are among the noble hallmarks of your traditions.[16]

The relationship of the Roman Catholic Church with Buddhism is deep. John Paul II has received the Dalai Lama five times at the Vatican, and has accepted his gift of a prayer shawl. It is in the United States that the Roman Catholic Church has taken Buddhism most seriously. There the Church has completely complied in respect to Buddhism with John Paul's insistence when he spoke in Rome on 3 March 1984 on the duty of religious dialogue:

No one can fail to see the importance and the need which inter-religious dialogue assumes for all religions of all believers, called today more than ever to collaborate so that each person can reach his transcendent goal and realize his own authentic growth and to help cultures preserve their own religious and spiritual values in the presence of rapid social change.[17]

The American periodical, *The Catholic World*, reported in its issue of May–June 1989 on a session of the International Buddhist-Christian Theological Encounter Group which took place in March of that year at Hsi Lai Temple, Hacienda Heights, California. This was the fifth meeting of the group, but the first to be hosted by a Buddhist community. Its topic was 'Buddha and Christ'. The twenty-five participants came from Thailand, Japan, Germany, Canada and the United States. *The Catholic World* commented:

One of the high points of the meeting was the celebration of a Christian service on the Sunday morning. We all realized that our meeting was deeply enriched by being in a Buddhist temple setting . . .

. . . The next meeting will focus on truth, reflecting one of the major points of conversation at the fifth meeting in Hacienda Heights. We – Christians and Buddhists together – will seek the truth through love, wisdom and compassion.[18]

The May–June issue of *The Catholic World* in 1991 was almost entirely devoted to the Roman Catholic–Buddhist connection. One of the contributors had an article drawing attention to the activity and theological position of Monsignor Vadakin, the director of the Office of Ecumenical and Interreligious Affairs for the diocese of Los Angeles:

Since the early 1970s . . . the archdiocese has been involved with the Buddhist community. . . . Msgr Vadakin also contributes through his office with the Episcopal Church, Lutherans, the Jewish Committee, the Islamic Center and others. This new exchange is an official, ongoing dialogue that includes Sri Lankan Buddhists, Thai, American Buddhists as well as Asian Catholics and those with Asian experience.[19]

The article concluded,

In summarizing the significance of this ongoing bilateral exchange, Msgr. Vadakin stated: 'The previous engagement between our communities had been singular and at a rather safe distance – and required little by way of risk, but now we have moved into a formal and ongoing relationship which allows us to join issues and test concepts. It also allows us to change perceptions of both the other and ourselves. I believe our experience has passed from overture to engagement, an engagement which contains much excitement and many suprises on the journey we have formally undertaken.[20]

Engagement means much more than dialogue; it means a commitment to one another. But this commitment has already been entered into. The article on the Hacienda Heights meeting contained, under a drawing of 'Manjurai, god of Wisdom', the words 'Given the level of understanding and trust that have developed over the last few years, the Encounter participants have agreed to try to leave time for worship, meditation and prayer'. One of the participants at Hacienda Heights was the theological heavyweight of trans-denominational importance, Hans Küng, whose acquaintance we made in the previous chapter.

John Paul II has also been intensively involved with the Islamic world. In February 1992, he visited Senegal, Gambia and Guinea. In Senegal he spoke of his gratitude to God for the numerous opportunities he had enjoyed during his pontificate to meet Muslim religious leaders and believers in Islam; he had received Muslim delegations at the Vatican, and enjoyed encounters with Islam on his apostolic journeys, especially in Africa. During his speech, he mentioned a message of May 1991 of the Catholic bishops of Senegal to all Christian denominations about the ongoing dialogue between Christians and Muslims, and how young people had united to build mosques and churches. He talked of 'a dialogue of life', a mutual acceptance, of mutual respect for freedom of conscience and worship, of the need for co-operation in creating a more just and free society. God was a God of dialogue, 'who since the beginning of time has been involved in a dialogue of salvation with the humanity he created, a dialogue that continues today and will go on to the end of time'.

But God is a God of proclamation, not of dialogue: 'Look unto me and be ye saved, all the ends of the earth' (*Isa. 45:22*). When God entered into a dialogue, it was with his own people, to ask them why they had not known or considered him: 'Come now, let us reason together' (*Isa. 1:18*). John Paul argued that Christians and Muslims both worshipped the same God, who 'is full of mercy for those who have strayed but turn to him in a spirit of humility and repentance'. But he ignored the fact that Islam has no concept of a sacrifice for sin as the basis for forgiveness. He ended with a prayer which made no mention of Jesus. He did indeed mention the Muslim regard for the person and work of Jesus of Nazareth, but that was not the main thrust of his address, which was on the need for dialogue, with a stress on what Muslims and Christians held in common. He spoke with warmth of 'a lovely letter' he had received from Hamid Algid, Secretary General of the Organization of the Islamic Conference, in which he had promised 'the availability of the OIC's member states to collaborate with the Holy See in advancing peace and strengthening the Islamic-Christian dialogue'.[21] In the same conviction that Christians and Muslims worshipped the same God, Cardinal Arinze of the Vatican Secretariat for Non-Christians, had in May 1988 sent a congratulatory letter to the Muslim world on the conclusion of the Ramadan fast.

The Roman Catholic devotion to the Virgin Mary has played a significant role in the convergence of Catholic Christianity and Islam, as well as Asian religions, particularly through the cult of Our Lady of Fatima, of which John Paul II is a devoted adherent. On 13 May 1917 three children began to see at Fatima in Portugal repeated apparitions of Mary, who is said to have identified herself as 'Our Lady of the Rosary' and to have charged the Roman Catholic Church with the consecration of Russia to her immaculate heart. John Paul believes his personal destiny to be directed by her, since 13 May 1981, the anniversary of her first appearance, was also the day he escaped an attempt on his life. Two shots aimed at his head had passed over him at the very moment when he had stooped to inspect an 'Our Lady of Fatima' medal worn by a little girl in the crowd celebrating the occasion. After a personal vision connected with Our Lady of Fatima, in obedience to her directive, John Paul II in 1982 consecrated Russia and the whole world to her immaculate heart. Since the development of the Fatima cult a remarkable phenomenon has occurred, partly because Fatima was the name of the daughter of

Mohammed, and as such venerated throughout the Muslim world:

When a 'Pilgrim Virgin', a statue of Our Lady of Fatima, toured Africa and Asia, millions flocked to venerate the statue and learn of Our Lady's 'Peace Plan from Heaven'. Muslims, Buddhists, Hindus and Sikhs were particularly enthusiastic. The Muslims, who have a certain devotion to Mary and recognize her Virgin Birth and Immaculate Conception, were intrigued by the fact that Mary had appeared at Fatima, which was the name of Muhammad's favourite daughter and regarded by the prophet as the highest woman in Heaven after our Lady . . . The Muslim Chief of the Ismaeli tribe in Mozambique placed a golden necklace about the statue's neck, saying, 'Thank you, Our Lady of Fatima, for the work of love you are accomplishing in Africa. We praise you, together with the Almighty Allah.[22]

Mary, the Mother, has a global appeal, since motherhood has always stirred the deepest longings of the human spirit. The place Mary holds in Roman Catholic devotion is rooted in the veneration of mother goddesses, often associated with the earth, in the Hellenistic world in which the church developed. A chapter in a standard text book of Hellenistic Religion, *Hellenistic Religions, an Introduction* (Luther H. Martin, O.U.P., 1987) is entitled 'The Mysteries and the Sovereignty of the Feminine'. In the modern world the earth to the Hindu is Mother Earth. Currently, those who are concerned with the future of the environment, have identified the Hindu Mother Earth with the mother of Jesus,[23] and we have arrived at full-blown syncretism.

The developments in the Roman Catholic Church represent a move towards syncretism rather than syncretism as such. Yet complete syncretism is already present there. It is to be found in a Hindu style guide to meditation, *Sadhana: A Way to God, Christian Exercises in Eastern Tradition*, the work of an Indian Jesuit, Anthony de Mello. It is published in the U.S.A. by the Institute of Jesuit Sources, St. Louis, Missouri. The cover of the book shows Jesus on the cross, with a meditating figure at his feet, legs crossed in the traditional lotus position, which the book recommends at the best posture for meditation. It also recommends the chanting of the Sanskrit word *Om*, especially for group meditation to the accompaniment of a gong. We saw in our second chapter the trouble which the recitation of the *Om* brought upon John Lennon.

The travels of Pope John Paul II continue to be occasions for inter-faith gatherings. After a visit to Papua, New Guinea, for the canonization of the first indigenous martyr, where he was greeted by traditional performers, the Pope went on to Sydney, Australia, where a ceremony was held which included not only twelve denominations, but Muslims and Jews. It was reported in the *Sydney Morning Herald* on 18 January 1995. Buddhists from China and Vietnam also attended. The spokesman for the Australian Federation of Islamic councils welcomed the Pope with the statement, 'We fully support his ongoing commitment to solidarity across all religions, to respect each other and live in peace and harmony on this beautiful planet.' Eighty Maori worshippers attended a subsequent ceremony for the beatification of the foundress of a convent. Religious convergence is the order of the day.

2: *The World Council of Churches*

Changing attitudes to the relationship of Christianity to other religions in the Protestant world at large can be most easily charted by surveying developments within the World Council of Churches founded at Amsterdam in 1948. Preliminary meetings were held in Edinburgh and Oxford in 1937, and in 1938 at Tambaram, Madras, but the establishment of the Council was postponed because of the outbreak of the Second World War. At Tambaram, the Barthian Hendrik Kraemer asserted the exclusiveness of Christianity in uncompromising terms: the Bible did not reflect man's search for a transcendent God, but God's free and unilateral approach to man. The biblical revelation was discontinuous with all human longings for a concept of God. While Christians were on the same level as all human beings, the biblical message was totally different in kind from man's religions. The task of Christian mission was the uncompromising proclamation of God's deeds of salvation in Christ. Under its first General Secretary, Dr W. A. Visser't Hooft, whose forebodings of the coming syncretism we have already noted, this remained the prevailing attitude. John Hick, the doyen of the pluralists, lamented this fact in the second Younghusband Memorial Lecture delivered in 1977:

Let us look first at the confessional end of the dialogical spectrum. Here the Christian, in dialogue with people of other faiths, speaks from his own conviction that God has entered decisively into human history in the person of Jesus Christ, the Second Person of the Holy Trinity incarnate, who has revealed the divine nature and purpose for man in an unique and unsurpassable way in comparison with which all other revelations must necessarily be secondary, in the sense of being incomplete, imperfect, or preliminary, or in some other way vitally inferior to the Christian revelation . . .

So long as this stance was dominant within the World Council of Churches, as it was until the end of the General Secretaryship of Dr Visser't Hooft in 1966, this great ecumenical agency refrained fron inter-religious dialogue. Since then, however, dialogue has become the order of the day.[24]

But even two years later, by the time of the Council's General Assembly at Uppsala in 1968, it had not made serious contact with other faiths. The report of that Assembly contained only two paragraphs on inter-faith dialogue. The Council's officials, however, regarded Uppsala as a turning-point because it marked a departure from Kraemer's view of mission as proclamation. The Assembly set up a Secretariat on Dialogue, and in addition introduced the concept of the unity of the church as a sign of the unity of mankind, which would necessarily involve coming to grips with its religions. The clearest indication of the Council's rejection of the binding authority of the Bible was given when at Louvain in 1971 it approved the report of its Faith and Order Commission, one of the bodies out of which it grew and which remained under its umbrella. This stated that the authority of the Bible came from its ability to make the word of God audible and thus bring men to faith, an understanding which reduces its authority to a subjective authority experienced when people hear God speaking to them through it. Some of the participants in the preliminary study groups which prepared the report thought it more appropriate to speak of the influence of Scripture rather than its authority. It was also argued in pluralist fashion that the Bible was culturally conditioned, and that contemporary inter-pretations would also be similarly conditioned by the current situation: 'situation-conditioned hermeneutic perspectives are inescapable'. Further, other books such as the writings of Augustine, Luther or some modern authority might produce an identical hearing of God.[25] The Louvain report mentioned only Christian authors but on its entirely subjective premises the sacred writings of other religions could be included among the books through which God might be heard to speak.

The real watershed came with the General Assembly of Nairobi in 1975 on the theme 'Breaking Barriers', although the years between Uppsala and Nairobi saw important developments described in the report of the Central Committee prepared for the consideration at Nairobi. In the intervening period, the history of salvation was progressively conceived as the salvation of the world rather than as the salvation of the church and the line between the two was increasingly blurred. At Nairobi, Philip Potter, the General Secretary, was to declare, 'I want to keep always before our minds the fact that the ecumenical movement is concerned with the oikumene, the whole human race as it struggles to discover what it means to be human in the purpose of God'.[26] The need of the church to show solidarity with humanity as a whole is the constant theme of the General Assemblies of the Council and of the meetings of the various sub-committees into which it is subdivided. The Uppsala Assembly set up a 'Humanum Studies Group' to study what it means to be really human in an age in which science and technology have put potentially dehumanizing powers into human hands, and noted that the growth of political consciousness had created a belief that men everywhere had a right to a truly human life and to share in the resources of the world.

In 1975 the Central Committee at Addis Ababa drew attention to the ways in which privileged groups used their power to deny the human identity of others. In such a situation it argued that the churches should develop the clues left us by Christ as the embodiment of transcendence in human life, as Emmanuel, God with us and for us and present in and suffering with humanity and its problems. Ways of theology had to be developed which would set Christians free to share more faithfully in the various struggles of men and women to become fully human; the activity of God embodied in Jesus Christ offered to those committed to him an understanding of what it is to be fully human. Borrowing a term from the theology of liberation, the report prepared for the Nairobi Assembly spoke of the growth of 'conscientization', man's awareness of his responsibility for mastering his own history, a Marxist view which runs counter to the biblical concept of the sovereignty of God, who works out from beyond history his purposes within history. The Council's 'Programme to Combat Racism' (1969), its world consultation on human rights (1974) and its conferences on 'Black Theology and the

Theology of Liberation' and on 'Sexism in the 70's' show its reponse to what it called the cries of the dispossessed, the powerless and the silent.[27] The stance of the Council in so many areas differed little from that of secular humanism, as Dr Edward Norman, then Dean of Peterhouse, demonstrated in his Reith Lectures of 1978. This consideration, however, must be tempered by the reflection that the Bible shows God to be no less opposed to man's inhumanity to man than to man's apostasy from him when he worships other gods. But the Council went far beyond an expression of solidarity with the oppressed when its Commission on World Evangelism organized a conference on 'Salvation Today' at Bangkok (1972–1973), which defined humanization in almost exclusively social, economic political terms and hailed Chairman Mao as a contemporary saviour. At Nairobi, there was no discussion on the Second Coming of Christ and eschatology was seen as realized in the struggle of the contemporary world for liberation and human development. The ideologies of unbelievers were considered as other living faiths with which the Council should enter into dialogue. A basic conviction of the World Council of Churches was that there could be no separation of the sacred and the secular. Christ was in all history, and more than ever all history was seen as salvation history. The church should therefore become involved in the world and its needs and problems, and on a global scale, because the world had become one and its needs and problems were global. The World Council of Churches was in all this of one mind with the pluralists and the papacy. The Christian mind had become imbued with a pragmatic humanitarianism at a time when its consciousness of its distinctiveness had been eroded by an increasing theological liberalism. Dialogue, not proclamation, was to be the order of the day.

In 1970, The W.C.C. held a 'Consultation on Dialogue between Men of Living Faiths' at Ajaltoun, Lebanon, in which Buddhists, Hindus and Muslims were brought together to meet with Christians for the first time. In spite of suspicions and misgivings, the participants expressed a sense of belonging and sharing. It was emphasized that the consultation was experimental, but dialogue was to continue and to develop further by involving other faiths, including Judaism and the African religions. At a meeting in Addis Ababa in 1971, the Central Committee issued a theological justification for dialogue: Christ freed us from spiritual isolation to enable us to enter into genuine dialogue with believers of other faiths so that he could fulfil his promise of leading us into all truth. Christ's statement, 'I am the truth' was obviously not sufficient for the W.C.C. The Bangkok Consultation of 1971–1975, where for the first time the representatives of another faith, the local Buddhists, were invited to give their explanation of salvation, the Consultation reiterated this statement with greater emphasis. The Holy Spirit, it asserted has at all times been leading all people into the fullness of truth and abundant life, and is therefore at work in the world religions. This standard claim of the inter-faith movement ignores the fact that John 16:3, 'The Holy Spirit will guide you into all truth', was spoken to the disciples, and in view of John 14:7, 'the Spirit of truth, whom the world cannot receive', cannot be given a wider reference. A key-note speech at Ajaltoun was given by Georges Khodre, the Greek Orthodox Metropolitan of Mount Lebanon:

Dr Khodre attacked the 'juridical dogmatism' of theologians who ignored other religions and argued that Christians must go beyond the idea of 'salvation history'. The life of God was the Holy Spirit who was not tied to any particular event or institution and who was at work in other religions. This understanding would enable Christians to enrich their own Christian experience from the manifold riches of 'a universal religious community' without abandoning their firm hold on Christ and his Church. It would help them to approach adherents of other religions as human beings, without any confessional sense of pride or superiority.[28]

Khodre's theme was taken up and developed further in a consultation, 'Dialogue in Community' held after the Nairobi Assembly at Chiang Mai, Thailand. Here it was maintained that salvation history was to be understood as nothing less than the totality of what Christ had achieved for the salvation of the human race. Even though Christianity has a special role and was in discontinuity with other faiths, it was also in continuity with them, because all religious men had a relationship with a transcendent All, and this personal faith was prior to all religious traditions. Christ was master of the whole universe and present in every aspect of human history and culture. He was not to be brought by Christians to other peoples, but his vestiges were to be traced among them. He represented the first fruit of a new humanity; his coming constituted a promise of a new humanity for all. The chief characteristic of dialogue is vulnerability, a readiness to be wounded. In a dialogue conducted in this spirit, the claims of Christianity to universal validity would receive a mortal wound. Dialogue should not proceed deductively from one's own tradition, but from the common ground shared with others, our humanity, and the focus of theological reflection should be the ethos of our relationships with men of other faiths, not our conceptions of them. No dialogue is possible on the basis of the position that salvation is exclusively in Christ.[29] No Christian knows Christ completely and must remain in continuous dialogue with him. Our understanding of him will be developed through dialogue with men of other faiths, because God has been inspiring all men to seek for him in many different ways. The fact that Christians see Christ as the absolute way does not mean that there are no other ways; in dialogue new and unfamiliar aspects of Christ may be revealed to us.[30] We must always remember the gulf between culturally conditioned theology and unconditional faith.[31] For this reason we must take into account the fact that the Christ we conceive of may not be the real Christ,[32] and refuse to limit him to our own human understanding of him.[33] Because he has been at work in other religions, we shall find that as we enter into dialogue with those of other faiths, he has gone before us.[34]

It seems inconsistent with this tenor of thought that we read in the report presented for the consideration of the General Assembly at Nairobi, 'If dialogue is to take the form of the Christian witness, it can never reach the point where the Christian has to confess to the other man, "I am as lost as you are; all we can do is to press forward together in our search for the truth." The Christian . . . will ever be conscious that he possesses a treasure and that treasure is Jesus Christ'.[35] The whole thrust of the W.C.C.'s position is that we are all engaged in a common search and pilgrimage. According to the Nairobi report 'We have to create a community of common searching'.[36]

The later Chiang Mai consultation told us that a Christocentric view of salvation does not do justice to other people's experience of God's favour[37] and, as we have seen, encourages us not to take Christ to others but to find his traces among them. It also asserted that without an acknowledgement that we are all searching there could be no fruitful dialogue.[38] In spite of the statement that Christians could never give up the treasure which they possessed in Christ, Bishop George Appleton, who was so involved in the World Congress of Faiths, suggested that dialogue would be helped if Christians concentrated on God rather than on Christ:

If God is the Creator of all, if he has made man in his own image, must we not think of him as coming to all, caring for all, trying to influence all in the direction of truth and goodness? This last question has a sharp challenge to Christians: have we emphasized God so much as Redeemer that we have neglected our belief in him as Creator?[39]

Many, but not all of the delegates to Nairobi, supported dialogue on the ground that other religions contains *logoi spermatikoi*, seeds of the truth,[40] a view dependent on the unacceptable exegesis of John 1:9, making Christ the universal enlightener, exegesis used in Vatican II as we have seen and in some utterances of John Paul II. At this stage in the history of the W.C.C., however, some delegates considered dialogue as a disguised form of syncretism. Dr Stanley Samartha wrote:

Serious confrontations between delegates did take place. There were some who considered 'non-Christian' religions as 'demonic' and were opposed to any form of dialogue or efforts at seeking community with them . . . Repeated allegations of syncretism put people on the defensive and side-tracked the nature of the community Christians need to seek in a multi-religious and multi-ideological world.[41]

Samartha was Director of the Programme on Dialogue with People of Living Faiths and Ideologies of the W.C.C. He leaves us in no doubt of where he stood. A dozen churchmen from Europe and North America, led by Dr Leonard, then bishop of Truro, and the Rev Eric Elliott of Ulster, left the Assembly in protest at the radical attitudes being forced on the delegates. The Nairobi Assembly in fact rejected the charge of syncretism;

dialogue does not promote syncretism, one of the delegates argued, but provides a safeguard against it because it leads to an in-depth knowledge of faiths and tests and refines one's own faith.[42] Nevertheless, in the history of the W.C.C. as a whole it represented a step towards syncretism. It was the first General Assembly to which representatives from non-Christian religions were invited, namely, Judaism, Islam, Hinduism, Buddhism and Sikhism. They were allowed to read short papers to the Assembly. The Hindu delegate was Professor K. L. Seshagari Rao, editor of *Insight*, the magazine of the Temple of Understanding, the U.S. counterpart of the syncretizing World Congress of Faiths. His contribution was to reprimand his hosts:

It is the exclusive and imperial attitude of some Christians that threatens the human community.[43]

This is a charge to which the W.C.C. has always been particularly sensitive. Its stance is that because their view of Christ is limited and culturally conditioned, Christians must enter into dialogue without any feeling of superiority. It is necessary to repudiate aggressive evangelistic crusades and to abandon the negative attitude to other faiths which have made Christian proclamation ineffective and irrelevant. The term 'non-Christian' is to be avoided because of its divisiveness, and no contrast is to be made between biblical and other faiths. The issue is no longer between 'The Gospel and Non-Christian Religions' or between 'The Word of God and the Living Faiths of Men', but the dialogue which must take place is to be 'Dialogue with People of Living Faiths and Ideologies'.[44] The faith of Christians and the sense of community in Jesus Christ which they have must never be allowed to strengthen the tensions and hatreds which threaten to tear the one family of humanity apart. This would be an abuse of faith for demonic purposes.[45] The latter statement, made as it is by those for whom the term 'demonic forces' has no literal reference, seems designed as a threat against evangelism; the former ignores the fact that the human family can only be united in Christ, who alone can restore the image of God in which all men were created, but which has been marred in all men.

The tenor of all these statements is that Christians cannot be trusted to evangelize sensitively in love. It is undoubtedly true that some nineteenth-century missionaries were culturally conditioned to think of the non-white races as lesser breeds without the law and tried to enforce Christian behaviour on new converts in the energy of the flesh rather than relying on the power of the Spirit, but this is the result of their insensitivity to the leading of the Spirit, and does not invalidate the claim of Christ to be the way, the truth and the life through whom alone men can come to the Father (*John 14:6*). It is simply not true that the exclusive Christ projected today, as the W.C.C. expresses it, is the product of the exclusiveness of heritage in which the church grew.[46] Some of the methods and attitudes of the early missionaries may have reflected the culture in which they grew, but the exclusive Christ they proclaimed was the Christ who claimed to be exclusive and whose claim was reiterated by the apostles: 'Neither is there salvation in any other: for there is none other name under heaven given among men, whereby we must be saved' (*Acts 4:12*). For this reason, it is illegitimate to distinguish between the exclusiveness of Christ and the exclusiveness of Christians.[47] Apart from the aberrations of some early missionaries mentioned above, in insisting on the exclusiveness of Christ, Christians are not showing themselves to be culturally conditioned; they are merely being loyal to the claims of Christ himself.

This line of argument would not be regarded as valid by delegates to the Chiang Mai consultation, who maintained that in this pluralist world it was more and more difficult to use the Bible as a criterion for evaluating the truth claims of other religions. For many of us, however, the Bible must always be the norm by which all religions must be assessed. According to Chiang Mai, the *Bhagavad-Gita* contained words similar to those of Jesus, and to Hindus it was the word of God. Such biblical truth as the historical particularity of Christ, the cross and the resurrection did not correspond to the Hindu concept of truth, and Christians had no right to judge Hindu spirituality. The Hindu mystic shows in his life qualities akin to what Christians call 'life in the Spirit'.[48] Instead of looking to the Bible, Christians must look back to the apophatic language of their own mystics.[49] With the W.C.C. we are once more up against the position of Thomas Merton and its endorsement by Dr Runcie. This is only natural; the *via negativa*, the denial that we can have a positive knowledge of God, is always a chief weapon in the arsenal of those who would marginalize Christ.

The attitude of the W.C.C. at this stage in its history towards syncretism was ambiguous. In spite of the demurrer we have just observed, the report prepared for the Nairobi Assembly suggested that apprehension about syncretism could be voiced too easily. Such fear was a stumbling-block to Asian and African Christian communities, and made them feel cut off from a creative relationship between their Christian commitment and non-Christian environment. We need to discover the revelatory elements which live within all cultures and take from them all that enriches.[50] At Chiang Mai one of the contributors was prepared for Christianity to assimilate the animism of African religion: the African heritage affirmed reality in the biblical sense because it accepted a spirit world as an integral part of the whole of human existence.[51] During the same consultation it was also argued that syncretism could be regarded too negatively; in some cultures there were those who in their alienation needed to seek help from many sources.[52] The most extraordinary proposal came from the Nairobi Assembly: the catechetical, liturgical and theological materials of the churches should be examined and revised by people of other faiths.[53] Non-Christians, that is to say, were to be called in to tell Christians what they ought to believe and how they ought to worship. This is akin to Hans Küng's suggestion that Christians ought to remould Christology in order to accommodate Islam.[54] Doctrinal issues apart, dialogue would get nowhere unless it were accompanied by shared religious experience and shared spirituality which, on an inter-faith level, must necessarily involve some degree of syncretism.

There can be no objection to inter-religious dialogue as such. But dialogue as envisaged by the W.C.C. is vitiated from the outset by the theory that all religious institutions, beliefs and writings are culturally conditioned. The corollary of this pre-supposition is that there is nothing absolute in Christianity which stands in the way of its adaptation to fit the milieu in which it is to be established. Such adaptation has come to be termed contextualization, which was the main theme of the Bangkok Consultation of 1972. Contextualization involves starting from the local situation and interpreting the biblical revelation in its light, instead of first going to the Bible and then seeing what it has to say about it. Contextualization has given us Black African, liberation and feminist theologies. Bruce Nicholls has provided an admirable critique of it in his *Contexualization: A Theology of Gospel and Culture* (Paternoster Press, Exeter, 1979). He shows there how the attempts of Third World and some Western theologies to find the fulfilment of the gospel in the beliefs and practices of other religions inevitably lead to syncretism. The endorsement by the W.C.C. of these theologies means that it is a syncretistic body. A non-syncretizing approach to contextualization follows a different path:

The evangelical . . . begins the process of contextualization with the unique and final revelation of God in Christ and the gospel which he interprets in the context of his own and the receiver's culture. To do this in a relevant way he must understand the cultural context and the questions which it raises. He must study both the Bible and the newspaper. But the process of theologizing is a one-way street. The gospel judges all of culture and not just some of it, destroying what is contrary to the Word of God and recreating what is true to God's universal revelation to mankind.[55]

God's universal revelation to mankind, it must be understood, is not the enlightening of mankind by the cosmic Christ, but the revelation given to man in his innermost being by the image of God in which he was created, and which, though marred, is still able to make him aware of God and of what God requires of him, though not to respond to him.

In his balanced and charitable book, *What About Other Faiths?* Martin Goldsmith has reminded us that the New Testament uses three terms which have the same root from which we get our English 'dialogue' – *dialogizomai*, *dialogismos* and *dialegomai*. The first two have the sense of questioning and uncertain thinking, the third that of arguing, reasoning and contending. In his Gospel, Luke uses the first two – Mary 'dialogued' in her mind about the angel's greeting (*Luke 1:29*), and the Pharisees questioned Jesus' teaching (*Luke 5:1–22*). But in Acts, he changes to the third to describe the confident teaching of the apostles. Advocates of dialogue commonly use Acts 17 in support. But the result of Paul's dialoguing ('reasoning') was that all the city was set in an uproar (verse 5). Goldsmith comments that we cannot imagine 'modern ecumenical dialogues producing such definite reactions'.[56] The W.C.C. has no intention that its inter-faith dialogues should arouse dissension. The 'dialogue' of the apostles was always accompanied by proclamation and aimed at conversion.

Since Nairobi, there have been two further assemblies of the W.C.C., one at Vancouver in 1983 and a second at Canberra in 1991. A report of developments since Nairobi was produced for the consideration of the Vancouver Assembly, and for the Canberra Assembly a similar report of developments since Vancouver. Both reports record dialogues with representatives of other faiths during the intervening periods, although the report of the Vancouver Assembly shows that inter-faith dialogue was still meeting with some resistance, as at Nairobi.[57] It would be a mistake to regard the W.C.C. as a monolithic body; it is not without an evangelical presence. The dialogues listed dealt for the most part with the pressing problems and evils of the contemporary world which have preoccupied the W.C.C. since its inception – the impact of science and technology, the need to establish a truly just and human society and the question of the whole future of humanity. These problems were discussed with Jews, Muslims, Hindus, Buddhists and representatives of the traditional cultures of Africa, Asia, the Pacific and the Americas. Closer ties were developed with the latter than during the previous history of the W.C.C. In 1987, at Sorrento in Canada, for the first time traditional elders from North America met with the W.C.C., and were allowed to set both the agenda and the style of the encounter. They expressed the conviction that dialogue which combined listening as well as talking would enrich the lives all participants.[58]

Three other meetings were of particular significance in the development of inter-faith thought. In 1980, one hundred and five people were brought together in Madras to the 'conscientized', in the term used by the report, about promoting inter-faith relations; the recalcitrant were evidently to be brought into line.[59] In 1988, at Toronto, fifty women from eight religious traditions met to discuss Scripture, tradition, leadership, authority and sexuality. They visited one another's places of worship, which they described as reinforcing the lessons learned from dialogue. Since by this time many Christians, as a result of the inter-faith movement, were incorporating in the practice of their faith meditative techniques and elements of worship drawn from the Eastern religions, the W.C.C. in the previous year invited thirty representatives of those who had adopted this way of life to a Consultation at Kyoto in Japan, the site of the World Conference for Religion and Peace in 1970.[60] One participant spoke of the 'astonishing multiplicity and particularity of God's incarnate presence' which she had found in Hinduism.[61] Another argued that Christ is too great to be reduced to the expression of him conveyed through the New Testament and the church: 'Thanks to all that his Hindu brothers and sisters have experienced on their pilgrim path, . . . we discover him as he truly is, always beyond all name and form, always beyond all his innumerable manifestations'.[62] As ever in religious pluralism we find a denial of the uniqueness of the incarnation. A third participant, who had belonged to Bede Griffiths' Saccidananda Ashram and had gone on to found another ashram of the same name following identical practices, spoke of 'the union of the divine and human in oneself'.[63] This interpretation of a mystical experience was expressed most starkly by another participant when she claimed that the ultimate religious realization is not the discovery of an objective truth but the personal discovery that 'I am He'.[64] In two communities from which delegates came the chanting of the Hindu *Om* was used. In one, it was combined with the Hebrew names of Mary and Jesus, *Om Mariam, Om Yeshua*.[65] In the other, it was preceded by the singing of a Hindu mantra, and prolonged into *Ommmmm* and later in the meditation into *Ommmmmmmm*.[66] The end of all these exercises is identical, the experience of 'the oneness of all in God' and 'the discovery of the Christ-Self'.[67] The final recommendation of the consultation was for the integration into Christianity of 'those elements of other religious traditions which help us and our church to grow together towards wholeness',[68] a recommendation reminiscent of the suggestion of the Nairobi Assembly that adherents of other faiths should be called in to help Christians in the revision of their creeds and liturgies. The whole report deserves more reflection than we can give it in this survey. Everything in it is evidence of the manner in which all inter-faith activity results in the reduction of Christianity and the marginalization of Christ, and that recourse to Oriental religions in particular calls us to recognize the God and the Christ already within us.

The Vancouver Assembly reflected the growing importance attached by the W.C.C. to the inclusion of the insights of the religions of primitive peoples as well as those of the more highly developed and familiar religions of the East. A native arbour, 'a sacred meditative area among the trees' was established on the site, and a sacred flame, lit by an elder of the Musqueam tribe, burned throughout the duration of the Assembly. A fifteen metre high totem pole, carved by native American prisoners to symbolize humanity's spiritual quest through the ages was raised on the site, and intended to find a permanent home in Geneva.[69] This could only turn eyes away from the Christ who is the sole answer to humanity's spiritual quest.

Vancouver marked a new departure in giving a central place to environmental issues alongside those of justice and peace:

To engage member churches in a conciliar process of mutual *commitment (covenant) to justice, peace and the integrity of all creation* should be a priority for World Council programmes. The foundation of the emphasis should be confessing Christ as the life of the world and Christian resistance to the demonic powers of death in racism, sexism, caste oppression, economic exploitation, militarism, violations of human rights, and the misuse of science and technology.[70]

This declaration inaugurated what has become known as the JPIC programme ('Covenanting for Justice, Peace and the Integrity of Creation'). The underlying belief for the necessity of such a covenant is that man now has the power to wreak such devastation upon the earth that it will be incapable of sustaining human or any other form of life. This ignores the biblical statement that when Christ comes again, human life upon the earth will be pursuing its normal course (*Luke 12:26–30*). It also ignores the fact that this earth is not forever; the time is coming when God will establish a new heaven and a new earth in which righteousness will dwell (*2 Pet. 3:10–13*). This does not mean that man is entitled to abuse the earth and ignore ecological considerations, or that such behaviour is not sinful. Christians may and must co-operate with men of good will and other faiths in promoting justice, peace and respect for the environment, but they can do so without participating in inter-faith activity. Above all, they must not embrace the paganism which is at the heart of most environmentalist thinking. Before Canberra, but with the issues to be considered at Canberra in mind, Anand Veeraraj, a presbyter of the Church of South India, wrote in an article, 'God is Green' in the W.C.C.'s *International Review of Mission*, Vol. LXXIX, No. 314, April, 1990:

There are those of us who seek a return to the lifestyle and values that reflect the ancient ecological and spiritual wisdom. Together we form a great household of faith as sons and daughters of Hirwa, the green god, and *Bhumi*, the Great Mother Earth.

Explaining that Hirwa, which means green, was the god of the Wali tribe in the jungles of Maharashtra, an area which had suffered from deforestation, and after quoting the hymn to Mother Earth in the *Artharva Veda*, one of Hinduism's most cherished scriptures, he concluded:

Real and lasting security, freedom, health, wealth and shalom will return to this earth only when Hirwa, the green god, the Logos of Creation, is raised to the highest place and given a name that is greater than any other name, and so, in honour of that name, all beings in heaven and on earth will fall on their knees and openly proclaim that he is Lord, to the glory of God (*Phil. 2:9–11*).[71]

He forgets that Jesus was accorded that name, because through God he humbled himself, became man and was obedient to death, even the death of the cross (*Phil. 2:6–8*). In such syncretism, the green god takes precedence over Christ.

Before the Canberra Assembly, the JPIC process was continued by a world consultation at Seoul in 1990, for which the Vancouver Assembly produced a study guide, *Between the Flood and the Rainbow*. The Seoul report, *Now is the Time*, is remarkable because its front cover contained a logo of a lotus flower in which a cross was inserted, and which was also printed on its last page. In Eastern religion, the lotus position is the normal position for meditation. The lotus flower also appears prominently in the New Age 'Great Invocation' a prayer issued by the New Age organization World Goodwill, and explained as a symbol of the heart or soul, the centre of the Christ-consciousness in man.[72] The W.C.C's choice of the lotus as the logo for one of its important publications is indicative of its turning away from Christ to the East, and an endorsement of the adoption by many of its adherents of the Hindu and Buddhist meditative practices which they unashamedly proclaim as the way to discover precisely this inner Christ-consciousness.

The Canberra Assembly began with a service in which its participants passed through smoke from burning gum leaves.[73] Responding to the criticism that this ceremony was syncretistic, the bishop of Bristol defended it in a letter to *The Times* of Wednesday, 11 February, 1993, on the grounds that it linked 'aboriginal culture with the Christian rite of purification', but its implication is clear: to those who devised and participated in it, the blood of Jesus Christ does not cleanse us from all sin (*1 John 1:7*), or at any rate, a little extra cleansing will do us no harm. Many of the delegates said that the Maori artwork on display remained their most vivid memory of the Assembly.[74] One visual aid used was of a cross behind which a writhing serpent was depicted. This was not a reference to the victory of the cross over Satan declared in Colossians 2:14–15; the serpent in aboriginal religion represents the Creator. One plenary presentation, 'Churches in Solidarity with Women', was built around the image of the 'greening cross'. A photograph was taken of a group standing around a cross which had a green shrub in the centre, as if Christ died for the environment and for the environment alone.

The second speech at the opening session was given by Chung Hyun Kyung, Professor of Theology at Ewha Women's University, Seoul. Addressing the Assembly theme, 'Come, Holy Spirit – Renew the Whole Creation', she began by invoking the spirits of the dead who had suffered injustice of one kind or another. Starting with the biblical characters Hagar, Uriah, Jephthah's daughter and the infants slain by Herod, she proceeded through a series of victims in later history to the spirits of contemporaries:

Come. The Spirit of Mahatma Ghandi, Steve Biko, Martin Luther King Jr., Victor Jara and many unnamed women freedom fighters who died in the struggle for the liberation of their people.

She went on to turn to the environment:

Come. The Spirit of the Amazon rain forest. Come. The Spirit of earth, air and water, raped, tortured and exploited by the human greed for money.

Her final appeal was to Jesus, but not to Jesus the Redeemer:

Come. The Spirit of the liberator, our brother Jesus, tortured and killed on the Cross.[75]

She referred to her own country as ridden with spirits full of *Han*, which meant anger, bitterness and broken-heartedness, but also the energy to struggle for liberation. Living people's responsibility was to respond to these spirits, through whom the Holy Spirit spoke 'her compassion and wisdom for life'.[76] All this ignores the biblical prohibition of attempting to contact the spirits of the dead (*Deut. 18:10–12*), and gives us a Holy Spirit who does not proceed from the Father and the Son.

The main impression of the Assembly on the Australian press was its proclamation of universal salvation. Its Director of Inter-Faith Dialogue, Dr Wesley Ariarajah was reported as saying:

It is inconceivable to me that a Hindu or a Buddhist, or anybody, is outside God. My understanding of God's love is too broad for me to believe that only this narrow segment called the Christian church will be saved. If you are a Christian, you must be open and *broad*, not narrow and exclusive.[77]

The view attributed to him here is consonant with what he wrote in a book for the W.C.C., *The Bible and People of Other Faiths*, the thesis of which is that Jesus did not claim to be the full, final and decisive revelation of God, and that it is difficult to see how such an exclusive position can be taken even on the basis of the Johannine verse, 'He who has seen me has seen the Father'.[78] Weighing the claims of Jesus, like Ariarajah, in the light of the whole biblical revelation, a contemporary New Testament scholar, N. T. Wright, comes to quite a different conclusion. He asks about Jesus,

Why should such a person, a good first-century monotheist, not also come to hold the strange and risky belief that the one true God, the God of Israel, was somehow present and active in him and even *as* him?

And what, we may ask, is so difficult about accepting for oneself that this claim of Jesus might be true? Aye, there's the rub. But that is perhaps what one should expect. Pearls of great price do not come cheap.[79]

For an adequate comment on the Canberra Assembly and on the whole position of the W.C.C. as it now stands, it is not necessary to go further than the reflections of the Orthodox participants:

The Orthodox note that there has been an *increasing departure from the Basis* of the W.C.C. . . . Its text is: 'The World Council of Churches is a fellowship of churches which confessed the Lord Jesus Christ as God and Saviour according to the Scriptures and therefore seek to fulfil together their common calling to the glory of the one God, Father, Son and Holy Spirit' (Constitution). Should the W.C.C. not direct its future work along these lines, . . . it would tend to become a forum for an exchange of opinions without any specific Christian theological basis. In such a forum, common prayer will be increasingly difficult, and eventually will become impossible, since even a basic common theological vision will be lacking.

The tendency to marginalize the Basis in W.C.C. work has created some dangerous trends in the W.C.C. We miss from many W.C.C. documents the affirmation that Jesus Christ is the world's Saviour. We perceive a growing *departure from biblically-based Christian understandings of*: (a) the Trinitarian God; (b) salvation; (c) the 'good news' of the gospel itself; (d) human beings as created in the image and likeness of God; and (e) the church, among others . . .

The Orthodox follow with interest, but also with a certain disquiet, the development of the W.C.C. towards the broadening of its aims *in the direction of relations with other religions*. . . . All this, however, must occur on the basis of theological criteria which will define the limits of diversity. The biblical faith in God must not be changed. . . . We must guard against a tendency to *substitute a 'private' spirit, the Spirit of the world or other spirits for the Holy Spirit* who proceeds from the Father and rests in the Son.[80]

This warning remains unheeded. John Bluck, an Anglican delegate from New Zealand, came away from Canberra saying, 'The question after Canberra will become not whether syncretism, but what kind', as if there could be different kinds of syncretism.[81]

One example of syncretism finding its unquestioned way into the W.C.C. was forthcoming soon after its Assembly at Canberra. In May 1994, one of its publications reported a conference for women held under its auspices at Minneapolis in the United States. The chief speaker was Chung Hyun Kyung, who as we have seen caused deep concern to the Orthodox Church at Canberra. After denouncing the churches for their patriarchalism and declaring the intention of women to destroy it, she explained how her Christianity had been transformed by three goddesses – the Hindu Kali, the Buddhist Kwan-Yin and the indigenous Ina of the Philippines. She further announced:

My bowel is Buddhist bowel, my heart is Buddhist heart, my right brain is Confucian brain, and my left brain is Christian brain.

The conference worshipped God as 'Sophia' taking wisdom as personified in Proverbs 8 and feminizing it because of the alleged importance felt by women of reclaiming feminine attributes for God. Inconsistently with this attempt of the conference to justify itself on semi-biblical grounds, Aruna Gnandason, an official of the W.C.C., stressed the need for women to 'look for values beyond just what has come down to us in the Bible'.[82]

3: *The Church of England*

The Commonwealth Day Observances are not the only inter-faith events which have taken place in Anglican churches. In 1984, there was an inter-faith service in Newcastle Cathedral in which Rama (the seventh incarnation of the Hindu god Vishnu) was worshipped as Lord, King and Lord of all. A Hindu idol was brought into the cathedral to the accompaniment of chanting, dancing and the offering of flowers. Muslims, Sikhs and Baha'is adored their own deities. The name of Jesus was not mentioned; the only specifically Christian element in the service was one line of a hymn: 'The Son and Him who reigns . . . in highest heaven'. Canon Peter Selby welcomed the congregation with the words, 'Religious people do not know what they believe until they pray and praise. And so in coming here today, we are glad to be celebrating our different traditions and in the process to be seeking for that which is the truth that binds us together'.[83] In the Chapter House of Bristol Cathedral there was a service in 1988, at which the Baha'is affirmed that all religions were one, and the Buddhists that salvation was to be attained through good works.[84] The Rev Robert Boulter, a Manchester clergyman, teaches in his Sunday morning services about Allah and Krishna alongside Jesus. Interviewed by *The Independent* on 13 July, 1992, he replied, 'People often ask me, "Has Christianity anything distinctive to offer?" I say, "No, it hasn't. I see no difference between Jesus and Muhammed in the terms of the message they bring us."'

These developments led the Church in 1992 to produce a report *Multi-Faith Worship? Questions and Suggestions from the Inter-Faith Consultative Group* (London, Church House Publications). This begins with the idea of the cosmic Christ in the sense of a universal revealer with which we are familiar. Here it follows the distinction made by Kenneth Cracknell in his book *Towards a New Relationship* between the eternal Logos and the historical Jesus; the eternal Logos or Word of God is independent from the historical man Jesus Christ, in whom it fully dwelt for a limited period.[85] Independently of its incarnation in Christ, the Logos is active as God's agent in revelation for all time. This concept of the Word, as we have seen, comes from an unacceptable exegesis of John 1:9.[86] Cracknell's severance of the Logos from Christ is also biblically untenable. While the incarnate Christ walked on earth, he continued to be God with God: 'no man hath ascended up to heaven, but he that came down from heaven, even the Son of Man which is in heaven' (*John 3:15*). Cracknell comes near to reducing the Logos, the second person of the Trinity, to a mode of God's existence, namely, his role as revealer and thus to reverting to the old heresy of modalism. Like all pluralists from Sir Francis Younghusband on he detracts from the uniqueness of the incarnation by describing the activity of God in Christ and in other human beings as one of 'immeasurable degree, not of absolute kind'.[87]

The report argues that the Old and New Testaments alike witness both to the universal activity of God and to his particular and unique activity in Israel and Jesus Christ, but finds that their authors repeatedly failed to appreciate its universal dimension.[88] We should honour both the uniqueness and universality of Christ and not play off one against the other. An unbalanced emphasis on the uniqueness and finality of Christ has narrowed people's vision of God's relation to the world and led them to exaggerate the distinction between the church and the world. Here a remark of James Denney is apposite: if we lose the only Christ we lose the only Saviour for all the world. It is hard to see in the light of Scripture how an emphasis on the uniqueness and finality of Christ can be unbalanced, unless we align ourselves with the 'Jesus only' Pentecostals, for whom the trinitarian God has disappeared. Scripture is unequivocal on this point, and it is appropriate to reiterate:

God, who at sundry times and in divers manners spake in time past unto the fathers by the prophets, hath in these last days spoken unto us by his

Son, whom he hath appointed heir of all things, by whom also he made the worlds; who being the brightness of his glory, and the express image of his person, and upholding all things by the word of his power, when he had by himself purged our sins, sat down on the right hand of the Majesty on high (*Heb. 1:1–3*).

The Bible is equally adamant on the distinction between the church and the world. The Old Testament declares, 'The Lord doth put a distinction between the Egyptians and Israel' (*Exod. 11:7*). The New Testament is just as categorical: 'They are not of the world, even as I am not of the world' (*John 17:14*).

As examples of God's revelatory activity outside Israel, the report cites the Melchizedek incident (*Gen. 14*) and the story of Balaam (*Num. 22–24*).[89] But Melchizedek, though a Canaanite priest-king, showed himself to be a true worshipper of Yahweh by acknowledging Abraham as a worshipper of the one true God. He clearly transcended Canaanite religion. Balaam was also a believer in Yahweh. The story of Naaman the Syrian (*2 Kings 5*), according to the report, ends with Elisha permitting Naaman to continue to worship Rimmon because of the social and cultural difficulties he faced. But Naaman became a true worshipper of Yahweh (2 Kings 5:15), and asks for his forgiveness in making a formal bow in the temple of Rimmon because of his high position in Syria. Elisha was silent on this point and did not sanction Naaman's proposed action. The incident cannot be used to justify inter-faith worship, and therefore much less to justify it on the ground that it secures better relations between different cultural communities, as the report also argues.

The most extraordinary statement of the report is its assertion that 'the Old Testament does not always look for conversion in a later Christian sense on the part of those who stand outside Israel, but rather for recognition and acknowledgement of Yahweh as the one true God, even while those who make the recognition remain within their own cultural and religious contexts'.[90] It places Naaman in this category, together with Jethro (*Exod. 18*), Nebuchadnezzar (*Dan. 4*), and the pagan sailors and people of Nineveh in the book of Jonah. This statement not only weakens the New Testament insistence on the need for the explicit confession of Christ, but also misrepresents the Old Testament. Naaman was converted to Yahweh and was apologetic about bowing to Rimmon, which had become a meaningless ritual to him. Jethro was a worshipper of Yahweh. Nebuchadnezzar recognized Yahweh's superiority in Daniel 4, but does not seem to have come to full and lasting penitence and Scripture is silent on whether the people of Nineveh made a long-term commitment to Yahweh. None of the examples given by the report justify the conclusion it draws from them. Throughout the whole of the Old Testament, Yahweh is pleading with his people to abandon their syncretistic ways.

The report makes much of Malachi 1:11, 'For from the rising of the sun even unto the going down of the same my name shall be great among the Gentiles; and in every place incense shall be offered to my name, and a pure offering: for my name shall be great among the heathen, saith the Lord of hosts'. The verb 'shall' is not represented in the Hebrew, but is supplied by the translators of the A.V. The report therefore denies that the verse has a future reference, relying on the R.S.V. 'is', which places the verse in the context of the time when it was written. It argues that Malachi is contrasting the formality of Israelite worship in the restored temple with the acceptable worship of the surrounding peoples from a pure heart.[91] It does, however, concede that other interpretations are possible. In her commentary on the book, J. G. Baldwin says, 'The Hebrew needs no verb, and whether the present or future tense is to be understood depends on the next clause. . . . "Incense is offered" represents a difficult Hebrew expression made up of two participles, but [the English versions] solve the problem by taking the form as a noun "incense", (i.e. that which is made to smoke). The second, also passive and causative, means "is caused to be offered", though the tense is flexible and not necessarily present . . . The context has to be the decisive factor. But even if the future is used, it has the sense "is about to be offered", indicating that the event is near at hand and sure to happen. There is therefore an eschatological element in this verse.' She continues that the adjective 'pure' is not used to describe Levitical offerings, and concludes, 'To maintain that pagans could offer pure offerings to God when the God-given sacrifices were not so described in indefensible'.[92] Malachi was prophesying a world-wide acceptable worship, which Jesus was about to make possible through his sacrifice on the cross. Such worship would not be dependent on the Levitical sacrifices. A strong case can be made for rejecting the report's interpretation of the verse and in view of the different understandings to which it is open, it is a shaky foundation for the validation of inter-faith worship.

The New Testament passages on which the report relies for its justification of inter-faith worship are also expounded erroneously. One is Paul's encounter with the Athenians recorded in Acts 17: 'Paul makes a positive evaluation of the "religiousness" of the Athenians. . . . Their religious traditions, it might be claimed, were in part a response to the calling of the unnamed, cosmic Christ, and as such were regarded by Paul as part of God's gracious preparation for the full proclamation of the Gospel. Paul's judgement did not entail a general positive evaluation of other worship traditions, so much as a spiritual discernment that the hearts of those he encountered in Athens were by no means entirely turned away from God by their religious observances'.[93] The facts are quite different. Paul was grieved by the prevalent idolatry in Athens (v. 16). He said that the Athenians were very 'religious' though the word could mean 'superstitious' as the A.V. has it (v. 22). He used the altar dedicated 'to the unknown God' as a point of contact (v. 23), but went on to declare that the one true God was a God the Athenians had never envisaged: he did not dwell in temples and did not need anything from man (vv. 24–25). He contradicted the Stoic pantheism of the Athenians and their Epicurean philosophy of chance (vv. 24–28). God had been patient with their ignorance, but now required their repentance (v. 30) as a preparation for the coming judgement to be executed by Christ (v. 31). Paul did not commend the religious observances of the Athenians, but summoned them to abandon them. The exegesis of Acts 17 by the report is misguided, and its conclusion wrongheaded. Paul's sermon points away from the legitimacy of inter-faith worship, not towards it. The remaining scriptural passages cited by the report are either equally misrepresented or irrelevant. A full analysis of them is given by the Rev T. Higton in his *Multi-Faith Worship?, A Critique*.

The report contains several provisos about the legitimacy of inter-faith worship. One is that 'it is neither appropriate nor lawful for words or actions which are contrary to the Christian faith to be performed in an Anglican church'.[94] Another reads, 'In their participation in such services, Christians should avoid giving the impression that Jesus Christ is merely one of many saviours'.[95] A third rules that 'the alteration of hymns in order to remove references to Christ, against the intention of the authors, is not acceptable'.[96] All these principles have been flouted in the Commonwealth Day Observances and in every other inter-faith service in the Anglican premises we have described previously, and also in the Canterbury multi-faith Service of Welcome to Pilgrims on Friday, 15 September, 1989, to be considered in the next chapter. Here the name of Jesus was excluded altogether.

CHAPTER IV

Environmentalism and Inter-Faith

1: *The International Consultancy on Religion, Education and Culture*

We saw in the previous chapter how the World Council of Churches was plunged into the environmentalist tide which has been engulfing the minds of concerned and sensitive people during the last two decades. It is now carrying the inter-faith movement in its wake. On 29 September, 1986, a month before Pope John Paul II summoned an inter-faith gathering at Assisi to pray for peace, the World Wildlife Fund celebrated its twenty-fifth anniversary under the aegis of its President, Prince Philip, Duke of Edinburgh, with a similar gathering in the same city. Five religions took part, Buddhism, Christianity, Hinduism, Islam and Judaism.

Buddhism was represented by the Venerable Lungrig Namgyal, abbot of the Gyuto Tantric College in India, the personal envoy of the Dalai Lama, Christianity by Father Lanfranco Serrini, Minister General of the Franciscan Order, Hinduism by Dr Karan Singh, President of the Virat Hindu Samaj, Islam by Dr Abudullah Omar Nasseef, Secretary General of the Muslim World League, and Judaism by Rabbi Arthur Hertzberg, Vice-President of the Jewish World Congress. The plan was to have five separate liturgies taking place simultaneously, but at particular points in the ceremony each faith was to present its own attitude to each of the five themes considered by the conference in the presence of the others. First came an act of thanksgiving for creation, followed successively by an act of repentance, a celebration of each faith's vision for the future, an act of dedication to implement these visions, and finally a sending forth of the delegates into the cultures from which they came. In addition, each faith was to issue a declaration of its attitude to the environment, but these were to be published after the celebration was over. The congregation processed from the convent of the Franciscans to the Basilica, while a muezzin chanted from the Bell Tower in praise of Allah. As it approached the Basilica, it was challenged by a Maori warrior to determine in the traditional way whether a visitor was coming in peace, but on this occasion the challenge was for all to take seriously the perspectives on nature of the indigenous peoples of the world.

It would take up too much space to describe the whole ceremony, but it will help us to highlight the elements in it which are at variance with the Christian faith. In the opening celebration of creation, a Hindu representative performed the traditional Hindu dance of creation, and then read from the *Creation Veda* a passage illustrating Hinduism's profound agnosticism about creation:

> That from which creation came,
> Whether well founded or not,
> He who sees from heaven above,
> He only knows, Or, He too knows it not![1]

In the act of repentance, the Buddhist delegate read a prayer written by the fourteenth Dalai Lama which referred to the ability of the Buddha to dispel the sufferings of man's cyclic existence, a clear reference to the Buddhist belief in the round of countless deaths and reincarnations necessary for man to reach *Nirvana*.[2] The Muslim representative read the Qur'an's account of the fall of man, which omits the biblical promise of redemption (*Gen. 3:15*).[3] In the celebration looking forward to the future, the Duke of Edinburgh gave an introductory talk on the significance of the Hindu *raksha*, a bracelet tied by sisters round the arm of the man who protects them, symbolizing the belief that, while the man offers physical protection, it is the woman who offers spiritual protection.[4] In the Bible, it is the man who is responsible under God for the well-being of the woman in all its aspects. The Duke's introduction was followed by the Buddhist envoy reading from the *Shantideva's Guide to the Bodhisattva's Way of Life* about the Bodhisattva's dedication to the salvation of others as the Buddhists understand salvation.[5] Here Buddhism parts company with biblical truth: 'None of them can by any means redeem his brother, nor give to God a ransom for him' (*Ps. 49:7*). The Muslim contribution to this section was a commentary on a brief text from the Qur'an, during which it was stated that Islam teaches the perfectibility of man;[6] the Bible asks, 'Who can bring a clean thing out of an unclean?' (*Job 14:4*). In the act of dedication the Hindu spokesman talked of the 'peerless Spirit that lies in all creatures', of 'the deathless Flame in living beings', an expression of the Hindu belief in the god within each being, the Brahman which is Atman:[7] the Bible tells us that man is alienated from the life of God (*Eph. 4:18*).

The declarations made by the representatives of their faiths' attitude to the environment all contain statements at variance with Christianity. The Buddhist declaration describes our existence as a 'spark of life' which we receive from a previously sentient being who or which is no longer alive (the reference to re-incarnation is obvious); beings so linked indicate the interdependence of all sentient beings throughout the whole universe.[8] Nothing is said about our creation by and dependence upon God. The Hindu declaration defines Hinduism as an encompassing world view which 'looks upon all objects in the universe, living or non-living, as being pervaded by the same spiritual power'.[9] Man, 'though at the top of the evolutionary pyramid at present, is not seen as something apart from the earth and its multitudinous lifeforms';[10] he is not, as in the Bible, the peak of God's creation. It also denies the transcendence of God: the 'divine is not exterior to creation, but expresses itself through natural phenomena'.[11] The earth is viewed as 'the Universal Mother' and 'we are all her children'.[12] It is therefore not surprising to read in a W.W.F. publication that at Assisi a twelve inch high puppet of 'Mother Earth' was carried through the streets. It is disconcerting, but perhaps not surprising, to be told that the puppet also represented the Mother of Sorrows and Mother Mary.[13]

The reason why the 25th anniversary of the World Wildlife Fund for Nature took the form of an inter-faith event is given by the *Radio Times* in its issue of 27 September–3 October, 1986. This reported that the Duke of Edinburgh became interested in bringing the different religions together to buttress the environmental cause when he read a W.W.F. sponsored book, *Worlds of Difference* by Martin Palmer and Esther Bissett for use in schools telling the creation stories of eight different religions. He brought in Martin Palmer, who in 1983 had founded his own religious and educational consultancy, the International Consultancy on Religion, Education and Culture (ICOREC), to organize the celebration on inter-faith lines in order to establish an alliance between conservation and the forces of religion. The aim of ICOREC was to promote a greater understanding of the religions and cultures of the world. Its activities rapidly became multifarious. It set up a Network on Conservation for the W.W.F., and took charge of Interlink, a World Council of Churches project on other faiths, as well as advising other sub-units of the W.C.C., on inter-faith issues. It also helped non-Christian religions to prepare their own educational materials not only for their own adherents but also for those of other faiths. In addition, it aimed at making available the sacred books of the various faiths and undertook the publication of occult works, namely, the books of Chinese astrology. It thus entered the vanguard of the inter-faith movement.

In view of the importance of ICOREC, it is necessary to understand Martin Palmer's theology, from which its whole activity stems. His major belief is that 'redemption is not just for humanity but for all creation'.[14] He bases it on God's covenant with Noah ('This is the token of the covenant which I make between you and every living creature', *Gen. 9:12*, cf. *v. 15*). But he ignores the fact that this covenant was made for man's sake (*Gen. 8:21*). More seriously, he ignores God's covenant with Abraham, which is far more important for salvation history, in which he promised him a seed through which all the nations of the earth would be blessed (*Gen. 22:17–18*). He argues that 'the salvation of humanity takes place within the salvation of all creation. Christ is sent to the world by God because, as the Gospel of John says, "God so loved the world that he sent his only begotten Son"'.[15] But he does not complete his quotation of John 3:16, omitting the rest of the verse, 'That whosoever believeth in him should not perish but have everlasting life', which shows clearly that the term 'world' does not mean the creation, but the world inhabited by man, and that God sent his Son so that men, not creation, could have eternal life. Palmer's key scripture, after the Noachic covenant, is Colossians 1:18–20, '[he] is the beginning . . . that in all things he may have the pre-eminence. For it pleased the Father that in him should all fulness dwell; And having made peace through the blood of the cross, by all things to reconcile all things to himself; by him, I say, whether they be things in earth, or things in heaven'[16] (I keep to the A.V., because the Greek word translated as 'fulness', *pleroma*, is in Jewish thought a technical term referring to Christ's complete divinity. The 'perfection' of Palmer's translation does not do justice to the text). He comments, 'Sadly, it has to be said that the Church has tended to lose sight of the fact that salvation was for "everything on earth" and has presented the atonement of Christ as basically of significance only to human beings.' He gives the passage a universalist sense which it does not bear. Bishop Handley Moule, a saintly scholar of an earlier generation tells us why:

Not without significance, surely, there is no mention here of 'the things under the earth', in the phrase of Phil. ii. 10. The world of loss was indeed in some undiscovered sense to 'confess that Jesus is Lord'; and that is an assurance which has in it, if we may say so, an awful peace. Let us not read into this passage what is not here, and is not anywhere in Scripture an absolute universalism, a 'larger hope' which is ultimately to neutralize the most formidable warnings. Let us be sure that God will be for ever and everywhere HIMSELF in His whole character; that He will never be inequitable and unmerciful. But let us pray for a holy fear, deep and awful; let us 'flee from the wrath to come'.[17]

The passages to which Dr Moule refers here are completely ignored by Palmer. Instead, he writes of an 'understanding of the end of the world' in which 'a sad and distorted hope has been expressed. The belief in "the elect" alone who would be saved. This has led people to wish for the end of the world in order to "teach them a lesson". It is a vengeful understanding, unfortunately fed by much in the Book of Revelation, but bearing little relationship to the Christ who died upon the cross and prayed, "Father, forgive them".'[18] This is a caricature of the attitude of those who believe in election, as one of them can testify. Robert Murray M'Cheyne (1813–1843), the pastor of St. Peter's, Dundee, kept his congregation in constant remembrance of Christ's tears over the lost, in which his followers must follow him; when pleading with the lost in the presence of his church members, he could say, 'There is not a child of God in this place that does not weep for you'.[19] A belief in election is central to the New Testament (*Rom. 8:29–30*; *Eph. 1:4*; *2 Thess. 2:13–14*; *2 Pet. 1:10*), and has always gone hand in hand with compassion for the lost and inspired intense intercession for them. Palmer has to excise key passages from the Bible in order to assert that it teaches 'a holistic idea of salvation and of at-oneness with God which stands as a constant rebuke to our self-centred belief that salvation is only for humanity'.[20]

For Palmer, the most serious sin, and the only one which is explicitly mentioned, is man's ill-treatment of the environment. Seven pages of his brief *Creation and Harvest Service Book* are devoted to it,[21] while man's sin against God gets only two mentions,[22] and his broken relationship with God is not mentioned at all. He expounds Matthew 5:23–24, where Christ was speaking exclusively about human relationships, as applying to man's relationship to nature: 'There is no doubt that the way we live and the demands which we make upon our environment mean that we are not reconciled with our brothers and sisters of creation. Seen in this light, how dare we come bringing the gifts of the earth as though we and we alone had right to them?'.[23] Having personified nature, he goes on to deify it: 'When we ask forgiveness of God, we know through his promises declared in Jesus Christ that we are forgiven if we truly seek to turn from sin. However, it will be many, many years before we will know if nature has forgiven us'.[24] Here he ascribes to nature a prerogative which belongs to God alone, the power to forgive. To deify nature in this way is to adopt pantheism. His interest in other faiths which prompted his book, *Genesis or Nemesis, belief, meaning and ecology*, springs from his belief that they do not encourage man to exploit nature as he thinks a thorough-going biblical faith does, a faith which he rejects for the same reason. It is all of a piece with his thinking that he endorses James Lovelock's *Gaia* hypothesis, that the earth is a living being, a single organism, capable of growth and development, containing within itself the conditions necessary for its own survival, which man disregards at his own peril.[25]

ICOREC has been responsible for organizing inter-faith events in three Anglican cathedrals – a Harvest Festival at Winchester on 4 October, 1987, a Creation Festival at Coventry on 9 October, 1988, and a three-day Festival of Faith and the Environment at Canterbury from 15–17 September, 1989.

The service book for the Winchester festival contained extracts from the writings of the Baha'is, Buddhism, Islam, Judaism, Sikhism and Taoism, which all present were invited to use as sources of prayer, inspiration and reflection. When the representatives of the faiths brought their harvest gifts to the nave crossing, they were halted by the Dean with a statement which expresses Palmer's beliefs without qualification: their gifts were unacceptable to God because of man's destruction of 'so much of Sister Earth' and his despoliation and slaughter of 'so many of our brothers and sisters in creation'. Before they proceeded further they were to listen to 'the voices of creation' (not of the Creator) describing in detail man's exploitation of the environment. The prayers of intercession and repentance had the same focus. 'Sister Earth' was declared blessed for providing our 'Brothers Wheat and Grape'. The call to repentance came almost verbatim from Palmer's *Creation and Harvest Service Book*: 'We need to ask forgiveness of God. We need to ask forgiveness of creation.' The Dean continued, 'As a priest, I can offer absolution from God for those sins for which we ask his forgiveness. Today we have to hope for forgiveness from Nature. We shall not know if Nature has forgiven us for many years to come. If we truly repent and our lives are changed and those of our contemporaries are challenged, then perhaps we shall have been in time.' Thus the Church of England took on board pantheism and Hinduism. The service ended when members of the congregation, consisting of members of other denominations as well as those of the other faiths, entered into a covenant with one another by tying on one another's wrists a rainbow coloured thread. The Dean introduced the ceremony with the declaration, again using Palmer's words, 'Now we need a new covenant. God's promise we do not doubt. It is humanity that we cannot trust. We hold the power of life or death. We have already swept away countless "living creatures that are found on the earth". Unless we change we, not God, will destroy life. Unlike God, however, we cannot bring to life again, nor can we create a new heaven and a new earth'.[26] The Director General of W.W.F. then invited the congregation to make the covenant:

We call upon you all to make a new covenant. We must now undertake not to destroy wantonly any living creature or damage life on earth to the point of extinction. The covenant is one between us and our neighbour and between humanity and nature. We invite all people of good will, whatever your faith or belief may be, to join us in the Rainbow Covenant.

After his brief explanation that the idea of the thread came from the Hindu *raksha* which had been used at the Assisi celebration, the congregation pledged themselves to the procreation of the environment:

Brothers and sisters in creation, we covenant with you and with all creation yet to be;
With every living creature and all that contains and sustains you;
With all that is on earth and with the earth itself;
With all that lives in the waters and with the waters themselves;
With all that flies in the skies and with the sky itself. We establish this covenant, that all our powers will be used to prevent your destruction
We confess that it is our own kind who put you at risk of death.
We ask for your trust
and as a symbol of our intention
we mark our covenant with you by the rainbow.
This is the sign of the covenant between ourselves
and every thing that is found on the earth.

The covenant was duly ratified by the tying of the threads.

Since Palmer thought this new covenant was necessary, one wonders whether he did in fact doubt God's promise. God's covenant with Noah and every living creature was unconditional, and therefore his promise is indefeasible. At the time when Christ returns before the inauguration of the new heaven and the new earth, human life will be continuing in normal circumstances on an earth which the environmental vandalism of man will not have made uninhabitable: 'as it was in the days of Noe, so shall it be also in the days of the Son of man' (*Luke 17:26*). That truth, of course, does not exculpate man's abuse of the environment. The first man was appointed to 'till' and 'keep' the

garden (*Gen. 2:15*). The word 'till' is regularly used in the Old
Testament in the sense of 'worship'. Man was created by God to
treat the world in which he was placed in an attitude of reverence
to him; it is never indicated that he was to take care of creation for
the sake of creation, as in Palmer's scheme of things.

It is unfortunate that Palmer should call his rainbow covenant
a new covenant. God has his own new covenant, and it is not a
covenant with creation, but, with respect to Palmer, a covenant
with man exclusively for man's salvation: 'This is my bood of the
new covenant, which is shed for many for the remission of sins'
(*Matt. 26:28*). It would have been more reverent if Palmer had
called his covenant with nature a novel covenant, to distinguish it
from the biblical covenant with which it has nothing to do.

The Coventry Creation Festival Liturgy contains a different
selection of extracts from the sacred writings of the same non-
Christians faiths, again offered as a basis for meditation and
prayer by all. It began with what purported to be a retelling of the
Genesis creation narrative in the light of modern scientific
knowledge. Outside time, it informs us, the consciousness of
God existed containing a thought of such intensity that it
produced the big bang from which everything that exists came to
exist:

> Our being is the expression of God's Thought.
> We contain the love of God and God contains us
> and as we unfold on earth
> through shell-creature,
> fish-form
> reptile,
> bird
> and mammal,
> through icthyosaurs
> plesiosaurs
> dinosaurs
> and ape –
> we are learning
> step by step
> what that containment means.

Apparently, God started off the big bang, and let the big bang
run its course; there were no further distinct acts of creation by

him. There is no reference to the fall, or even to a ruptured relationship with God. The sin from which protection is prayed is not a sin which separates us from God but the sin of our separation of ourselves from the rest of creation, 'the Great Work'. But as we are, 'Our being is the expression of God's Thought. We contain the love of God and the love of God contains us'. This is nearer to the Hindu conception of the *Brahman* which is *Atman*, and the *Atman* which is *Brahman* than to the biblical distinction between Creator and created. Later in the service, man and the earth cry out to God to be saved from destruction, not to be reconciled to him by the blood of his Son. After this, not God, but our 'brothers and sisters of creation' are petitioned to save us. As in the Winchester Festival, in the prayer of absolution, the celebrant of the eucharist said that as a priest he could offer us the absolution of our sins from a reconciling God, but could not offer us reconciliation with nature. The communion service contained the blasphemous words, 'On the night that Jesus was betrayed, he took bread, work of human hands, gift of the Mother Earth.' Even if the blasphemy was not intended, it is there. In Hindu thought 'Mother Earth' is a goddess. As we continue, the concept of the church as the body of Christ is thrown overboard: 'Though we are many, we are one creation because we all share in the love of the Creator.' The new creation in Christ Jesus is beyond Palmer's ken. In the offertory procession, a local conservation group brought a tree to the accompaniment of a beat symbolizing the heart beat of creation, 'a vulnerable and delicate sound'. At the same time, children of the cathedral's Junior Church carried a cross of nails. One gets the impression Martin Palmer was thinking of the crucifixion of nature, of which he speaks frequently. The cross of nails was described as 'a symbol of the broken made whole', hardly an adequate understanding of the atonement. It is also important to remember that in the Hindu declaration on the environment trees are classed as sacred and associated with the gods.[27]

The Canterbury Festival of Faith and the Environment, taking place over three days, was planned on a larger scale. It began on a pilgrimage on Friday, 15 September, 1989, from three centres, Winchester, Coventry and Watford, converging on near by Humbledown, where others were invited to join. The three groups were led by a Baha'i, a Christian and a Hindu. During the weekend there were Jewish, Baha'i, Dikh and Buddhist celebrations, and a Muslim call to prayer. On the Saturday, the children's group sang 'Yanomamo', the world's first ecological musical containing a number, 'Run Away ', with a chorus which began, 'The trees have power. We worship them. We live because they give us life. Yanomamo'. Exhibitions were on display in the chapel and cloisters by, among others, the Amaravati Buddhist Centre, the Baha'i Community and the Beshara Magazine. A workshop was held on Creation-Centred Spirituality (an admirable characterization of Martin Palmer's religious beliefs, but specifically associated with the Dominican Matthew Fox, of whom more shortly). Another was arranged by the Amaravati Buddhist Centre and Chithurst Buddhist Monastery, and another was entitled 'Shintaido', a practical workshop on stress management and self-healing (which clearly would not consider the peace of God which passes all understanding, or the healing which comes from God). The programme also included an 'Earth Healing Ritual', the title of which reveals its occult nature. The cathedral staff maintained that its involvement was 'in a totally Christian capacity'. The organizers' brochure described how the cathedral opened the cloisters for 'all faiths . . . to use the spaces for exhibitions, workshops, displays, art, drama, and music to express their concern for all nature'. The archbishop's chaplain wrote on behalf of Dr Runcie, 'There is no multi-faith taking place over the week-end.' But, as we have seen, trees were worshipped in Hindu fashion. During the opening service of welcome for the pilgrims, the Dean addressed the multi-faith congregation in true pluralist and World Council of Churches style as 'pilgrims together through the world of the Lord of Light'. Writing in 'The Christian Herald' on 30 September, the Rev Tony Higton rightly commented, 'The order of service . . . contains no hint of reference to Jesus at all. It was a carefully edited liturgy which removed all traces of Christian teaching which would offend or challenge other faiths.' The Sunday morning communion booklet included texts from Baha'i, Buddhist, Confucian, Hindu, Muslim and Sikh writings as resources for reflection, as is always the case where Martin Palmer is at work. During the festival all these faiths were free to distribute recruiting leaflets. When the Rev Tony Higton and fifty companions attempted to distribute Christian literature in the precincts, the cathedral authorities threatened to bring in the police to eject them. So at Canterbury, from the 15–18 September, 1989, it would seem, to adapt a phrase of Dr Visser't Hooft, all religions were equal, but the Christian religion was less equal than the others.

2: *Teilhard de Chardin's Theology of Evolution*

In the thought of Martin Palmer and the activities of ICOREC, with nature given the divine prerogative of forgiveness, we are confronted with what has become known as creation-centred spirituality, particularly associated with the Dominican Matthew Fox. But Fox's creation-centred spirituality is to a certain extent foreshadowed and certainly influenced by the thought of a Jesuit of an earlier generation, Teilhard de Chardin, whom Fox quotes frequently. In *Human Energy* (Collins, London, 1969), de Chardin proclaimed 'Humanity has reached the biological point where it must either lose all belief in the universe or quite resolutely worship it';[28] the universe is henceforward to receive the homage in traditional Christianity reserved for God. Worship of the universe is what we have discovered in the liturgies produced by ICOREC. What we have to resolve is whether in de Chardin's theology any room is left for the worship of God, or whether the worship of the universe takes its place. A first pointer to a solution is contained in another statement from *Human Energy*:

No spirit (not even God within the limits of our experience) exists, nor could structurally exist without an associated multiple, any more than a centre without a circumference. In a concrete sense there is not matter and spirit. All that exists is matter becoming spirit; the 'stuff of the universe' is spirit-matter.[29]

'Matter becoming spirit' gives us a three-word summary of de Chardin's whole thought; it suggests immediately that his universe is a material universe on its way to becoming a spiritual universe, a transformation involving God himself. But we must probe further. He describes this evolution as a progression from pre-life to life, from life to consciousness, from consciousness to reflective self-consciousness, from self-consciousness to super-consciousness, in which the energies of mankind coalesce into a collective human organism stretching over the whole planet, and finally from super-consciousness to the merging of everything that is into the Omega point, which is God. The process is gradual but punctuated by critical points at which the earlier stages suddenly break through into the higher.

The end, however, was there from the beginning. As spirit-matter the universe is fundamentally personal, and to guarantee both its personal character and also to guarantee the emergence within it at the end of its evolution of super-personality in the Omega point, it must have been personal from the beginning (though never of course as pure spirit without material embodiment). The final summit of a personalized world cannot be conceived of as born of an aggregation of elementary personalities. In de Chardin's terminology, in order to super-animate, that is, to confer more abundant life and higher personality on existing personalities, this final summit must be a separate centre in itself, guiding from its start the course of evolution from within. In this view, de Chardin believes that he has not only found room for the traditional concept of God as exercising his influence over individual entities separate from himself (he calls these 'monads'), but that he has based it solidly on contemporary evolutionary theory, and saved it from being merely sentimental or an emotional prop. Because it is tied up with evolution religion is not a matter for individual consolation or conviction but concerned with the collective destiny of humanity,[30] and is of cosmic significance.

De Chardin explains:

We have followed the cosmic spiritual phenomenon *from within* by the path of immanence. But now by the logic of this path itself, we are forced to turn and recognize that the current which elevates matter must be conceived rather as a *tide* than as a simple internal pressure. Multiplicity ascends, attracted and engulfed by something which is already one.[31]

His conception of God is ambivalent. In another context he tells us that his thought had not reached the idea of a God who depended only on himself for his existence,[32] and we may add that it never did so, for although *Human Energy* is a collection of early essays, it already contains the fully developed system we find in *The Phenomenon of Man*. Repeating the argument we have just followed, he asserts that the future term of the cosmos must be considered as having already attained the absolute by something in itself, and here he speaks of God's transcendence. God is a special term at the end of the series, but in some sense out of the series, having in itself its own consistence. In it everything climbs as to a focus of immanence, but everything descends from it as from 'a peak of transcendence'.[33] Although he thus applies the impersonal pronoun 'it' to God, as he continues, he again refers to God's personality: to be capable of acting on the wave of personality which its influence raises, God, the centre of centres, must already have a personality superior to the one it evokes.[34] In the context of de Chardin's whole thought, however, the mention of transcendence must be construed as a token nod to the orthodox God of Christian biblical tradition. Since the Omega point has not yet absorbed matter into itself, and nowhere in the present stage of evolution do we encounter pure spirit, we have at the moment only an immanent God.

This conclusion is reinforced by de Chardin's definition of Spirit. The Bible tells us God is Spirit: de Chardin tells us Spirit is a cosmic state of change.[35] It would therefore be fair to say that for him the Spirit is nothing more than evolution. Consistently with this interpretation he describes the stages of evolution as 'spiritualization'.[36] Its sphere is circumscribed by the universe, because its dimensions are those of the universe, neither more nor less.[37] It was there in the beginning, a network of consciousness,[38] not a recent accident, but a deeply rooted phenomenon reaching back as far as the eye can see[39] a tension on the surface of the earth,[40] a description far removed from the biblical statement that the Spirit moved upon the face of the waters (*Gen. 1:2*), leading to the critical point of the animation of matter, which until then possessed only the rudimentary consciousness of 'pre-life',[41] with the consequent appearance of the 'biosphere', the sphere of life, and of the 'hominization' of the biosphere with the arrival of man and his self-reflective consciousness, which produced the 'noosphere', the sphere of mind. It will be there in the future, taking us from 'personalization' to the 'monocentrism' of the Omega point, when the All becomes self-reflective upon a single consciousness.[42] In this final stage Christianity reveals its monistic character; the term is de Chardin's; he offers his work as a contribution 'towards Christian monism'.[43]

In monism, the Creator/creature distinction disappears, and we arrive at pantheism. De Chardin himself speaks of his 'profound tendencies towards pantheism'.[44] Pantheism is demanded by a cosmic sense, which is a sense of love in which the boundaries between the 'I' and 'the others' disappear, while the thoughts, feelings and actions of individuals melt into a single motion of apprehension, comprehension, passion and action, for multiplicity vanishes in the psychic domain.[45] It is required by Christianity, the essence of which is a belief in the unification of the world in God,[46] as the coalescence of all beings into God, achieved under the influence of love, when God will be all in all (*1 Cor. 15:28*).[47] But there is nothing in that phrase to suggest that Paul meant that the elements of the world or human personalities, as de Chardin also expresses it, would be fused or absorbed into God; he was looking forward to the time when the supremacy of God would be made manifest. De Chardin dares to call this fusion of the elements of the world in God as the birth of God, which does not consort well with what he has told us elsewhere about God being already there from the beginning. But it is another pointer to the exclusively immanent nature of his God.

We have looked at the course and outcome of evolution as de Chardin envisages it. We may also usefully examine how he conceives the mechanism of evolution. He distinguishes two kinds of energy, tangential and radial energy. Tangential energy is familiar because it surrounds us. It is external and therefore de Chardin calls it 'the without'. It is subject to the dissipation which scientists term entropy. Radial energy is internal and spiritual or psychic, 'the within'. It tends to complexity, possesses purpose and consciousness, and provides evolution with its direction. Unlike tangential energy, it leads to the convergence of all things, not their dissolution. In the beginning, the inchoate consciousness of elemental matter brought about the formation of more complex molecules. The increase of complexity led to a higher level of consciousness and to a greater degree of convergence, which led in turn to a still higher level of consciousness which intensified the process of convergence, and so finally evolution attains the Omega point.[48] There is here an implicit identification of radial energy with God. De Chardin's God is thus discovered to be definitively and irretrievably immanent. He is the 'within' who absorbs 'the without'. De Chardin's theology has more in common with Hinduism than with Christianity. The 'within' within 'the without' of the individual is the *Atman*, which through a sometimes gradual, sometimes sudden process of convergence, becomes one with the all-pervading *Brahman*. Like Hinduism, de Chardin's theology is both monistic and pantheistic.

As in all creation-centred theology, little is said in de Chardin's system about the relationship of the individual with God. If man is already through his 'within' connected structurally with the Omega point of the Godhead, he cannot have a personal relationship with it. Further, if man could have a personal relationship with the Godhead, it would be a collective, not an individual relationship. For before the Omega point is reached men have to attain to a collective humanity and a collective consciousness. Individualism is infantile and self-centred. Men must arise above the lesser groupings of family, country and race, and come together and increase their powers of acting as a crowd.[49] The convergence of men into a collectivity is the next stage in evolution, and is already visible in the manifold and ever more universal groupings taking place before our eyes.[50] It is demanded by our relationship with the earth and with the universe, and is both an expression of and a step towards the development of a spirit of the earth.[51] The most valuable part of a man's personality is what he is still expecting from the unrealized part of the universe.[52] We need to open our hearts wide to the call of the world within us and to cultivate a sense of the earth, which de Chardin defines as a passionate sense of a common destiny that draws the thinking fraction of life ever forward,[53] and as an irresistible pressure which unites men in a common enthusiasm.[54] There is a new principle of universal affection among the mass of living beings, a devotion of one element for another within a single world in progress.[55] The age of nations has passed. Unless we wish to perish, we must shake off our prejudices and build the earth; there is no biological future for the world except in an active consciousness of its unity.[56] The contemporary expression for de Chardin's thought would be the need to develop a global consciousness. This process of unification and collectivization is forced upon us by the very form of the planet in which we dwell[57] and, alternatively expressed, by the attraction of God.[58] When we remember that God is the 'within' of every 'without', de Chardin's terminology is coherent. God is structurally embedded in the constituents of the planet, and is thus its form. The form or structure of the planet and the attraction of God are one and the same thing. There is no room in de Chardin's theology for an individual relationship with God. God is not concerned with the individual, if a form or structure can have a concern, but with humanity collectively. Here de Chardin is explicit. Religion is not for the individual, but is the collective experience of the whole of humanity as God reflects himself personally in the organized sum of thinking monads.[59]

De Chardin continually asserts that the process of convergence and unification which constitutes evolution is indefeasible and irreversible. He nevertheless tells us that it can be resisted. Men mistakenly fear that their individuality will be lost by being pressed into a common mould and that their identity will perish by their entry into a collectivity, and therefore oppose the onward march of evolution. They fail to realize, in one of de Chardin's repeated phrases, that 'union differentiates', that it enhances their distinctiveness (he never explains how), and cling to the isolation which gives them their individuality. They set their faces against the good, which de Chardin defines as everything that brings spiritual growth to the world, and a fortiori against both the best, that which assures the highest development of the spiritual powers of the earth, and also the ultimate good, that which makes for the growth of the spirit on earth.[60] To de Chardin, morality consists in co-operation with evolution, understood as the continuous transformation of spirit-matter into the pure spirit attained at the Omega point.

Resistance to the stuff of the universe, spirit matter, was successfully carried through at an early stage in evolution by the rocks:

We may say that it is the characteristic of minerals (as of so many organisms that have become incurably fixed) to have chosen a road which closed them prematurely in upon themselves.[61]

The first sinners, therefore, were the first rocks, not the first man, (in an essay of 1924 de Chardin repudiated the biblical doctrine of the fall), the rocks which chose the wrong road. The good rocks were those which performed their evolutionary duty and became the megamolecules capable of forming the variable patterns required to make the critical breakthrough from pre-life to life. The sinful rocks were those which formed crystals capable of growing only to a set pattern. Man is not to emulate the crystals but the obedient rocks which opened themselves to the next stage of evolution. To write in this way is not to caricature de Chardin, for he seriously asserts that all duty originates in the atom.[62] If morality has anything to do with atoms, it can only be because atoms can obey or disobey.

For most men to co-operate with evolution will be too painful. They will therefore cling to their individuality and fight against collectivization. Only an élite will be able to lead us to the future:

The world of tomorrow will be born out of the elected group of those (arising from any direction and class and confession in the human world) who will decide that there is something big waiting for us ahead, and give their life to reach it.[63]

Evidently the amount or force of radial energy, 'the within' driving us on to the Omega point varies from man to man; only in a select few does it possess irresistible power. Men thus differ in their structure. De Chardin is not the systematic or rigorous thinker he is so often represented to be.

The nearest parallel to his whole way of thought is not to be found in Christian theologians but in a Hindu philosopher, Sri Aurobindo (1872–1950), who taught that divine energy was to be found everywhere, exercising its influence in both a descending and an ascending order. It descends through three layers of reality, a higher plane of infinite consciousness, an intermediate level of supermind and a lower layer of mind, life and matter. It then ascends, integrating each plane with the higher plane. As in de Chardin, we have the successive transformation of matter into life, or life into consciousness and of consciousness to superconsciousness, ending in complete identity with the Absolute, corresponding to de Chardin's Omega point. As in de Chardin, it would be an élite who would initiate and fulfil the process of salvation for all.

We have yet to examine de Chardin's Christology. As a beginning, we may say simply that he places Christ in the procrustean bed of evolution – to be the alpha and omega, Christ in his humanity must become co-extensive with the physical expanse of time and space.[64] The important thing is that 'Christ must become'; he is part of the evolutionary process. There is no suggestion that he is greater than the universe, that 'He is before all things, and that by him all things consist' or are held together (*Col. 1:17*). In order to reign on earth, he must 'super-animate' the world: 'in him, and by the whole logic of Christianity' (we may insert, as de Chardin views Christianity) 'personality expands (or rather centres itself) till it becomes universal'.[65] He is the God of progress and evolution,[66] leading us to the Omega point at which he has become co-extensive with the universe:

Christ, principle of universal vitality because, sprung up as a man among men, put himself in the position (maintained ever since) to subdue under himself, to purify, to direct and superanimate the general ascent of consciousness into which he inserted himself. By a perennial act of communion and sublimation, he aggregates to himself the total psychism of the earth. And when he has gathered everything together and transformed everything, he will close in upon himself and his conquests, thereby rejoining, in a final gesture, the divine focus he has never left. Then, as St. Paul tells us, *God shall be all in all.*[67]

There is no mention here of the Word made flesh; Christ is impersonalized, for all de Chardin's insistence on the personal character of the universe, as the 'principle of personal vitality'. Nor is there any question, at this stage of de Chardin's evolutionary Christ, of a finished work of Christ in the biblical sense. De Chardin, however, does speak of the incarnation; for him it is 'the Redeeming Incarnation', which he defines as a prodigious biological operation',[68] 'biological', possibly, because the disobedient inorganic rocks placed themselves outside its scope. Yet there may be hope even for them, because for de Chardin there is no individual but only universal salvation; being is by nature holy, and there is no salvation except of everything that exists.[69] It is significant also that according to de Chardin it is the incarnation, in the limited sense in which he understands the term, not the cross which redeems. Evolution involves groping, pain and failure, but all these are part of its onward thrust; the sufferers of the world join their sufferings so that they become a great and unique act of consciousness, elevation and union, of which the cross is the consummation.[70] We are therefore to avoid seeing the cross as the individual suffering of one who by it made a single act of expiation.[71] Its only uniqueness is as a symbol and place of an action the intensity of which is beyond expression. The cross of Christ is to be fitted into the totality of human suffering; it is in this context that he 'bears the weight and draws ever higher to God the universal march of progress'.[72] Modern scientific knowledge, our understanding of evolution, frees us from seeing the incarnation in the traditional terms of 'juridical symbols'.[73] Only now are we able to understand Christianity aright:

The essential message of Christ, I should say, is not to be sought in the Sermon on the Mount, nor even in the drama of the cross; it lies wholly in the proclamation of a 'divine fatherhood' or to translate, in the affirmation that God, a personal being, presents himself to man as the goal of a personal union.[74]

But in human experience fatherhood does not entail a personal union, nor is it a goal for the future; a man becomes a father as soon as he begets a son, and though father and son can enjoy a paternal-filial relationship, they do not become one person. In the teaching of Christ man knows God as Father, not at the culminating point of evolution, but in the here and now in the moment he accepts his Lordship. Nor does Christ offer men the union with the Father which he himself possessed as the second person of the Trinity. The unity of believers with the Father and himself for which he prayed in his high-priestly prayer (*John 17:21*), was a unity of fellowship, not a substantial unity. The incommunicable attributes of God can never be communicated to the creature.

De Chardin was a pluralist as well as a theologian of evolution: these two strands in his thought belong together. He wrote the inaugural address for the founding of the Union des Croyants, as the French branch of the W.C.F. was called. Members of the W.C.F. attended the inaugural meeting of the Teilhard de Chardin Association of Great Britain and Ireland in London in 1965. De Chardin wrote 'A Hymn to the Universe' for a thirty-two faith gathering, including Judaism, the Baha'is, Buddhism and Islam, held in Canada in 1967. He described the W.C.F. as holding the hope for the future of mankind.

3: *Matthew Fox's Creation Spirituality*

Martin Palmer and ICOREC urge us to save the environment. Teilhard de Chardin tells us to worship it and the whole universe. Matthew Fox, a Dominican who in 1977 established his 'Institute for Culture and Creation Spirituality', calls on us to celebrate the universe. His principal writings are *A Spirituality Named Compassion* (1974), *On Becoming a Musical Mystical Bear: Spirituality American Style* (1976), *Whee! We, Wee, All the Way Home, A Primer in Creation Spirituality* (1981), *Original Blessing* (1983), *The Coming of the Cosmic Christ, The Healing of Mother Earth and the Birth of a Global Renaissance* (1988) and *Creation Spirituality, Liberating Gifts for the Peoples of the Earth* (1991). We shall draw on all these to consider the relationship of his theology to our theme, the connection of the inter-faith movement and the New Age. His theology is highly heterodox, and earned him firstly the suspension of his right to teach in the Roman Catholic Church and ultimately his expulsion from the Dominican Order. This, however, is unlikely to diminish his influence any more than the initial papal ban on de Chardin's writings lessened his. He has now found a new platform as a priest of the Episcopalian Church in the United States.

Fox does not talk about inter-faith or religious pluralism, but he continually stresses the need for 'deep ecumenism',[75] by which he means the same thing. Nothing pleases him more than when his theology is understood to be identical with a non-Christian faith. He took it as a compliment when a Taoist called one of his lectures pure Taoism because Taoism reflects his own vision of cosmic harmony.[76] On another occasion a lady in his audience complimented him on his fluency in Hindi. He replied he thought he had been speaking in English. The lady, a Hindu, explained that in listening to him she had heard a pure exposition of Hinduism, her own faith. This was a just comment for Fox pointed to Hinduism as a religion where his Cosmic Christ could be found.[77]

But unlike Bede Griffiths and Thomas Merton, Fox finds spiritual renewal for himself not so much in the Eastern religions as in the native American tradition:

Praying with native peoples has always been a source of deep spiritual renewal for me. Sweat lodges and powwow dances, pipe ceremonies and vision quests are just some of the ways that have been employed by native peoples for tens of thousands of years on this land. Last year, . . . I had the privilege of praying with Lakota peoples at a Sun Dance in South Dakota. It was a deep spiritual experience . . . The Cosmic Christ is present in so many ways in the Sun Dance and its surrounding prayer forms – the sweat, the pipe giving, the vision quest. . . . The fire at the centre of the tepee, or of sweat lodge represents *Wakan-Tanka*, the Great Spirit within the world. How close this comes to Meister Eckhart's statement that an *ancilla animae*, a 'spark of the soul', burns within every creature and every human . . . and . . . this spark of the soul is the divine presence within us all. All of creation shares in this holiness.[78]

In thus reaching out to an indigenous religion, Fox is in line with the Canberra Assembly of the W.C.C. His interest in primitive religion was by no means confined to that on his own doorstep. Deep ecumenism, he believes, should also take into account all the pre-patriarchal religions of the world, such as the African and Celtic religions and the matrifocal Wikke or Wicca, ordinarily known as witchcraft.[79] It was his respect for the latter which led him to appoint to the faculty of his Institute for Culture and Creation Spirituality the witch Miriam Simos, who writes under the name of Starhawk, of whom Constance Cumbrey wrote in her book *A Planned Deception, The Staging of a New Age Messiah* (Pointe Publishers, Michigan, 1985), 'Miriam Starhawk is one of the world's most politically active and important witches. She is a high priestess in a major coven and has been involved in both the witches/Neopagan Movements as well as the feminist movement. She is a frequent speaker at New Age convocations and conferences'.[80] Fox has no objection to her on the latter count, for he includes New Age mysticism among the sources from which the new global spirituality must draw.[81]

Even these brief comments are enough to show that Fox belongs to the inter-faith and pluralist camp and have given us yet one more indication that the inter-faith movement and the New Age movement are connected. Before we turn to examine his theology it will be useful to juxtapose two passages from one of his earlier books which show the extent to which he believes that traditional Christianity has outlived its usefulness. He is convinced that a new age requires a new religion:

One tradition that offers a glimpse into our own futures . . . is the astrological tradition.

In particular, Jung subscribes to the way of seeing human history in 2000-year stages corresponding to the Age of the Bull (4000–2000 B.C.), a symbol of primitive instinctual civilizations and represented by Cretan religion; the Age of the Ram (2000 B.C.–1 A.D.), characterized by the religions of the Jews and the emergence of conscience and awareness of evil wherein religion sacrificed rams, the Age of Pisces, the fishes (1 A.D.–1977 A.D.), dominated religiously by the figure of Christ . . .

There is an extremely important *Caveat* that looms on our journey. That is the warning not to look back. . . . If you recall, when Moses came down from his experience with God on the mountain top he was so infuriated by what he saw the Israelites doing that he broke the commandment tablets. What were they doing? They were whoring after the past gods! They were worshipping the religion of the previous age, the Age of the Bull. They refused to face the new spiritual consciousness that Moses issued in, that of the Age of the Ram.

So we, too on the verge of breaking into a new spiritual age, need to beware of the Gods of the past. . . . We have a clear lesson from the Israelites: to look back piningly is to commit idolatry.[82]

It is remarkable to find one who claims to be a Christian appealing to Jung and astrology to support his position. It is even more remarkable to note how Fox has completely misunderstood the biblical narrative; the Israelites were not looking back to any past gods – they were breaking the covenant they had only just made binding themselves to the worship of Yahweh alone.

So we turn to Fox's theology. The first step towards the new religion which the New Age requires is to abandon the transcendent God who is over and above creation and, though immanent within it, is distinct from it in his transcendence. Fox quotes Jung again: to believe in a God out there, a transcendent God, is to lose your own soul.[83] Instead, we are to embrace panentheism, which Fox defines as the belief that God is in everything and everything is in God. Here the subject – object distinction between God and creation disappears.[84] We thus escape dualism, stemming from the separation of ourselves from all else, which is to Fox the 'original sin and the sin behind all sin'.[85]

All theisms are guilty of making this separation and are therefore to be jettisoned. In panentheism, the belief that creation 'is in God and God is in creation',[86] we avoid the dichotomy. After following Fox so far it is odd to discover him rejecting pantheism because it robs God of his transcendence, but then we find him saying that pantheism and panentheism are not so far apart and both are to be recommended because they both equally remind us that 'God is as much Mother as Father';[87] it is important to Fox that we should recognize the feminine side of God. Both in any case give us a purely immanent God; panentheism destroys the transcendence of God as effectively as pantheism. Panentheism is the less familiar of the two terms; it was invented by the process theologians, according to whom God created the world in order to develop himself further by responding to the reactions of creation to himself. Their God is thus an incomplete God, as we shall discover Fox's is.

We need now to enquire more closely into his conception of God. His regular term for God is Dabhar, the Hebrew for 'word', referring to all verbal communication and in the plural often denoting the law of God. Without any lexical or theological justification Fox translates it as the creative energy of God:[88]

In the beginning was the Creative Energy. The Creative Energy was with God and the Creative Energy was God.[89]

But since his God is purely immanent, the creative energy of God is a misnomer; Fox's Dabhar can only be the impersonal energy at work within the universe, which is how many New Agers view God. Further, since we are part of the universe, Dabhar is within each one of us, and thus we have the New Agers' God within. But though his Dabhar is impersonal, Fox constantly endows it with personal qualities: she (he invariably refers to God with the feminine pronoun) loves, delights in and perpetually plays with creation. It (or she) wants to become incarnate in all of us, as it was in the

divine incarnations birthed from the soil. Isis and Hesiod, Buddha and Lao Tzu, Moses and Isaiah, Sara and Esther, Jesus and Paul, Mary and Hildegard [a twelfth century mystic by whom Fox set great store], Chief Seattle and Buffalo Woman.[90]

There is thus nothing unique about the incarnation. Fox here aligns himself with all the pluralists. When we consider his use of the term we begin to wonder whether his theology has the right to use it. He explains it as follows.

This 'Son of Adam, Son of God' (*Lk. 3:38*) fully incarnates the Dabhar, the ever-flowing Cosmos-filling creative energy of the Creator. Yet he becomes fully flesh as we are, pitching a tent in our midst. Thus God is not incarnated as the Perfect One, but, since Jesus is 'alike us in every way save sin', as the imperfect one. The divinely imperfect one, or if you will the Imperfect Divinity. Here lies the scandal of the imperfections and limits of God and how badly God has need of us.[91]

This harmonizes completely with his concept of an incomplete God, but not with the biblical description of the Word made flesh. Christ is not the incarnation of the self-existent God, but of Dabhar, the immanent creative energy of the universe. We ourselves have to give birth to God, by allowing Dabhar, already active within us, to become fully incarnate in us.[92] Further, there is nothing intrinsically divine about Christ; he is divine only because of his personal qualities as a man. According to Fox, Jesus was not good because he was God, but God because he was good. He explains further:

Jesus is not so much compassionate because he is divine as he is divine because he is compassionate. And did he . . . not teach others that they too . . . were divine because they are compassionate.[93]

The consequence of such reasoning is to undermine still further, if that indeed is possible, the uniqueness of the incarnation. A compassionate man, and even fallen man because of his retention of something of the divine image in which he was made, can be compassionate, and can therefore be an incarnation of God.

Dabhar, or God, will not be complete until every one is incarnate, when the cosmic Christ will at last appear:

Essentially there is only one heart – the heart of the Cosmic Christ who is also the Bodhisattva, one who is fully committed to the enlightenment of every creature on earth.[94]

Again Fox reveals himself as one of the pluralists: they also sometimes find in Christ a Bodhisattva figure.

We have seen that Fox often speaks of the cosmic Christ, but have not examined what he means by that term. In part, but only in part, he means the universal enlightener of whom the pluralists speak when they mistakenly interpret John 1:9 in a Hellenistic sense.[95] He quotes several New Testament passages to show that Christ is ruler of the cosmos, but these only evidence the normal Christian belief that Christ will be Lord of all, but do not indicate that he will be voluntarily accepted as Lord by all, so they do not give us a Cosmic Christ in Fox's sense. He derives his concept of the Cosmic Christ above all from the Wisdom literature of the Old Testament and Apocrypha, and he uses the term as a virtual synonym for cosmic wisdom: 'the Cosmic Christ was present in Israel and in the Hebrew Bible principally as cosmic wisdom'.[96] Interestingly and significantly, because it reveals the extent to which he thinks of God as mother, he finds the origin of the Wisdom literature in the Egyptian worship of Isis: 'a black mother goddess' is 'behind much of this biblical literature'.[97] He does so on the authority of Rosemary Ruether, a feminist contributor to *The Myth of Christian Uniqueness*.[98]

At the outset of his book on the Cosmic Christ, he quotes her as saying, 'Wisdom is seen as the all-encompassing divine ground of being out of which the Trinity emerges. It creates the World, guides it to perfection, and unites the creation with the Creator. . . . Wisdom is the ground of being of the three persons of God'.[99] There was a god before the trinitarian God, more powerful than the trinitarian God, and her name was Wisdom. The new age to be ushered in by the Cosmic Christ will be the age of wisdom: 'If the Cosmic Christ has the power to come again in the hearts, minds and bodies of the humans on this planet, then surely that Christ will come as wisdom wakened, sought after and celebrated'.[100] Fox has no vision of the Pantocrator, the ruler of all things, as the Orthodox Church so magnificently names Christ, who is to come again regardless of the ability of human beings to make his coming possible. The Cosmic Christ is none other than cosmic Wisdom. Fox explains that he prefers the term 'Cosmic Christ' to 'Cosmic Wisdom' because he is writing from within the Christian tradition (a claim his whole theology nullifies) and one has to be loyal to one's own tradition (would that he had been). 'The term "Cosmic Wisdom"', he tells us, 'bears most of the meaning of the term "Cosmic Christ"'.[101] Again, 'Wisdom is the key to the Cosmic Christ . . . and it is evidence of a Cosmic Christ tradition long before Christianity'.[102] Thus 'Buddhism boasts its own tradition of cosmic wisdom. Like its western counterpart Sophia, this tradition speaks of wisdom as female – she is the "Mother of all Buddhas" who is teacher and nourisher of compassion. She is immeasurable and incalculable and deep like space itself, yet she is also "the ground of being".'[103] Thus Fox's Cosmic Christ is identical with Buddhist concepts. Once again, we have the adherent of inter-faith.

Once more we see that for Fox, as for all the pluralists, the incarnation of Christ is not a unique event. In the strictest sense, his theology has no incarnation. In the same way, the traditional doctrine of a substitutionary atonement is discarded; it is part of the old religion which has to be abandoned to make way for the new religion which is required by a new age. It is an unfortunate legacy from the fall–redemption tradition against which his strongest polemic is directed and which his creation spirituality is designed to replace.

As he sees it, to discuss the cross apart from 'the context of creation and incarnation . . . invites severe distortion of the Good News'.[104] The truth is that he is at a loss what to make of the cross. Negatively, it is not an appeasement of God;[105] positively it is the ultimate symbol of letting go,[106] the detachment to be found in Zen which his creation spirituality requires. But it can be interpreted in other ways. It is part of the cosmic pain of all nature on its way to rebirth;[107] it was a lost gamble;[108] it was a disastrous and premature death.[109] Ignoring all that Scripture says about the cross, Fox tells us it caused Jesus to lose out: 'no one can ever bring back the time that Jesus lost and will never live out'.[110] But the Bible teaches that Jesus did not die before he had finished the work God gave him to do (*John 17:4*). His life and death were all in God's timing. 'When the fulness of the time was come, God sent forth his Son, made of a woman, made under the law, that we might receive the adoption of sons' (*Gal. 4:5*), and the death of Jesus was in 'the determinate counsel and foreknowledge of God' (*Acts 2:13*). He died with the triumphant shout, 'It is finished' (*John 19:30*). Most idiosyncratically of all, Fox transfers the crucifixion of Jesus and its significance from the historical Jesus to the crucifixion, as he terms it, of Mother Earth in our own time, which he actually and not figuratively identifies with Jesus:[111]

I am proposing that in a Cosmic Christ context the paschal mystery takes on new power, deep meaning, and moral passion when we understand it as the passion, resurrection and ascension of Mother Earth conceived as Jesus Christ crucified and resurrected and ascended. It is, then, the life, death and resurrection of Mother Earth.[112]

The concept of the motherhood of God permeates his writings. The implicit evaluation of the crucifixion of Jesus as less sinful than man's exploitation of the environment lay behind the 'greening cross' at the Canberra Assembly of the W.C.C. and is also shared by Martin Palmer and has shaped his ICOREC liturgies. In concluding this study we shall examine Palmer's thought more closely and therefore reserve our comment on how the Christian must regard this view until we do so.

Fox's rejection of a unique incarnation and of a substitionary atonement (which he shares with all supporters of the inter-faith movement and which, as the two unique factors of Christianity, the religious pluralists are bound to abandon) is part of his wider attack on the fall–redemption tradition in theology which we need to examine more closely before addressing ourselves more directly to his creation spirituality. According to Fox, the fall–redemption pattern has for centuries weighed down theology, the conception of the fall of man and the initiative taken by God to redeem him. Fox maintains that this latter is a late perversion of original Christianity, the brainchild of Augustine (354–430), whose influence pointed Christianity to the wrong direction it has followed ever since. There never was an ideal original state, and death was not the result of sin, but is part of the order of nature, which continually goes through the cycle of life, death and transformation.[113] Concentration on sin is anthropomorphic, because sin entered the world only with humanity (was there not some original sin after all?); for billions of years before the arrival of man, creation was permeated only with blessing and Dabhar, God's creative power.[114] We ourselves do not enter this torn and sinful world 'as blotches on existence, as sinful creatures, we burst into the world as "original blessings"'.[115] Concentration on sin leads into cynicism and lack of compassion.[116] It trivializes sin by blinding us to the sins which most threaten our world, the sins of genocide and the most original sin of all, the danger of a nuclear holocaust, and leads to an increase of pain, injustice and sadomachism and to a contempt for creation and those who love creation.[117] It expresses dualism, the dichotomy between subject and object, and introduces fractures and fissions in all our relationships, manifested in war, rape and theft, which all result from our regarding the other as an object outside ourselves.[118] It teaches us to ignore remediable social evils,[119] and plays into the hands of empire-builders, slave-masters and the upholders of patriarchal society in general.[120] It is indeed the expression of patriarchalism, and lacks the wisdom of matriarchal societies which have always understood the interconnection of all things, the sole basis of compassion.[121] All these evils which Fox ascribes to the fall–redemption tradition in theology are collective evils affecting the whole of humanity. Nowhere does he indicate any awareness that these collective evils result from the accumulation of the countless individual sins which spring from every human heart, and that they are the expression of the original sin which he explicity denies. They do not have their root in a doctrine, but in man's innate sinfulness.

The catalogue we have given does not exhaust the list of evils from which Fox holds the fall–redemption responsible. It does not trust in existence, in the body, in society or in the creativity or in the cosmos, but is an expression of fear – the fear of damnation, of our own nature and that of others, of originality and of the cosmos itself, and denies the very ethos of religion, which was meant to be based on a psychology of the ever-growing expansion of the human person[122] which could be described in other terms as the full development of human potential. It transforms the search for holiness into a quest for perfection, which is egoistic and stunts our personal growth, or in Fox's phrase is 'not a deeply spiritual quest of the human person'.[123] It damages not only the individual but society, because it ignores the truth that it is our very imperfections which unite us and make us into a social organism the parts of which are concerned to help one another; it is shared weakness and need which draw from a group its gifts and power of healing.[124] Above all it trivializes the gospel, reducing it to the slogan 'Jesus saves'.[125] Individual salvation is in fact impossible, because man in his depth is a social creature. Salvation therefore must be holistic; man can only be saved in depth when society, the totality of mankind, is saved.[126] Fox here is as adamant as de Chardin. Later he describes what he terms 'privatized salvation' as a sin against the cosmos;[127] it brings into it the dualism of unsaved/ saved and fallen/redeemed.[128]

In all this Fox has the whole of Scripture against him. It just will not do to ascribe the fall–redemption tradition in theology to Augustine. Paul tells us, 'As by man's disobedience many were made sinners, so by the obedience of one man, many shall be made righteous' (*Rom. 5:19*). Jesus, speaking to men at their very best as self-sacrificial parents, could say, 'If ye then, being evil, know how to give good gifts unto your children, how much more shall your Father which is heaven give good things to them that ask him?' (*Matt. 7:11*). It is also idiosyncratic of Fox that he should characterize fall–redemption theology as anthropomorphic. Sin concerns man's relationship with God, apart from which it has no meaning: to sin is to fall short of the glory of God (*Rom. 3:23*). Nevertheless, Fox insists that men should turn from the 'egological consciousness' of the fall–redemption tradition to the 'ecological consciousness' of creation spirituality.[129]

Released from the burden of guilt, the hangover of the fall–redemption tradition, and realizing that where Dabhar is, there is no curse (*Gen. 3:17*) but only blessing, we are free to embark on the fourfold path of creation spirituality: the Positive Way of awe, wonder, and mystery of all beings as words of God, the Negative Way of embracing our pain and the pain of others which makes us compassionate, the Creative Way of co-operating with Dabhar and the Transforming Way of relieving suffering and combating injustice.[130] The four paths are Fox's substitutes for the purgative, illuminative, and unitive paths of traditional mysticism, so we may expect to find his creation spirituality imbued with a mystical element, which it is, but with the rejection of all the ascetic practices associated with traditional mysticism. Creation spirituality is celebratory and has no time for repentance in the ordinary sense. It is about relating ourselves to all that is, to

all beings, all things, the ones we see and the ones we do not, the whirling galaxies and the wild suns, the black holes and the microorganisms, the trees and the stars, the fish and the whales, the wolves and the porpoises, the flowers and the rocks, . . . the children we give birth to and their children and theirs, and theirs, and theirs[131]

and to all sorts of conditions of men and all the phenomena of the natural world.[132] It is the recognition that we belong to an interdependent and interconnected universe. There is no mention in Fox's definition of any relationship with God as such. This lack is even more evident in his statement that creation is 'our common parent, when "our" stands for all things'.[133]

Creation spirituality enables us to rejoice in the blessings of our earthiness, our sensuality and our passions.[134] We remember that Jesus was 'as earthy, as sensuous and as sexual as ourselves'.[135] Fox does not deny the virgin birth, but it is much more important to him that he was of the earth, earthy like ourselves.[136] We take delight that we are part of this interrelated cosmos, a cosmos which is moving, dancing, vibrant and full of surprises.[137] To live in this way is to live cosmically (not, be it noted, unto God), and it is within the power of all, because man is a cosmos in miniature, a microcosmos within a macrocosmos,[138] that is, he is made in the image of the cosmos. We also learn not to take thought for the things of the morrow. In the words of Jung, commenting on the Taoist text, 'The Secret of the Golden Flower':

The art of letting things happen, action through non-action, letting go of oneself, as taught by Meister Eckhart, became for me the key to opening the door to the way. We must be prepared to let things happen in the psyche. For us, this actually is an art of which few people know anything. Consciousness is for ever interfering, helping, correcting and negating, and never leaving the simple growth of the processes in peace.[139]

This quotation shows Fox's deep-rooted antipathy to all logical thinking and ratiocination. It is now commonly supposed that the left lobe of the brain is in charge of our analytical and verbal processes and the right lobe of our intuition, artistic imagination and mystical tendencies. Western civilization has come to be dominated by left brain activity and to ignore the right brain so that our educational system concentrates on mathematics, the sciences and languages at the expense of art, drama, dancing and music.[140] This applies also to theological training, so that it makes no attempt to cultivate mystical ability.[141] Instead, the emphasis is on doctrine and the fall–redemption tradition is its outcome.[142] It is impossible to teach creation spirituality 'within the confines of Cartesian, left-brained, academic structures alone'.[143] So Fox concludes:

Left-brain-itis is a lethal disease that today has quite literally the power to destroy all the earth. The right brain's contribution of feeling and connection-making, of mysticism and cosmic delight, of darkness and sensuousness needs to be taught and appreciated. Education needs to include the discipling and motivating of the right as well as the left brain.[144]

It is because of his insistence on the importance of non-rational right-brain thinking that he appeals so much to the mystics without any regard to the content of what they say.

In creation spirituality, the right brain comes into its own, because it calls for the artist and the mystic: 'art-as-meditation becomes the basic prayer form in the practice of creation spirituality'.[145] On this path we move from the cosmos to cosmogenesis, of which we are called to be agents, because the cosmos is still in birth.[146] We are to add new dimensions to it through birthing new images and giving effect to them.[147] We are made in God's image and have been vested by God with the divine power of creativity.[148] We are no less than co-creators with God, and are indeed more than this; we are divine. Fox here appeals to Eckhart, according to whom an image not only has one being with that of which it is the image, but is the same being.[149] Creativity is usually considered the special province of the artist, but we need to discover the artist in all of us, and to trust in our creativity.[150] But art needs the assistance of religion, without which it is sterile; it is the task of spirituality to make artists of us all. We become artists in the silence of meditation, which would be intensified with the bodily aid of deep breathing, and by avoiding the left-brain habit of expressing ourselves verbally. Images would then well up from the depths of our being.[151] We might find them disturbing because they would be new and could be disruptive of our peace, but we must trust them because the power we humans have to give birth is not only the divine power of the universe, but that of the divinity itself.[152] Further, the pain they bring is the pain of new birth and new creation, and is therefore salvific and healing. It leads us into new relationships with others (we need to remember that for Fox separation from the interdependent whole is the original sin), and even into the experience of transcendence.[153] Accordingly, 'we need to ride our images as one would ride a great eagle, soaring up and down wherever they take us.'[154] This is the letting go of which the Zen masters have reminded us.[155] In following the Creative Way we restore to the universe the beauty that was there before the sense of the cosmos was lost.[156] Leaving the fall–redemption tradition behind, we become instruments of divine grace and beauty, and channels for 'the Holy Spirit to spiral beauty back into the world through us'.[157] We also join the communion of saints 'which is the community of beauty-birthers', Fox's idiosyncratic defini-tion of the church. By restoring harmony to the universe, 'we are truly co-creators with the God of the cosmos.'[158] Fox does not remember that at the same time God promised not to curse the ground (his beloved earth) for man's sake, he made the pronouncement that 'the imagination of man's heart is evil from his youth' (*Gen. 8:21*).

Finally, creation spirituality recognizes that the planet has become a global village, which requires us to build a new civilization worthy of our dignity as royal persons and of our responsibility as co-creators with God.[159] In this civilization, peace and justice will reign, in which we shall be able to delight and celebrate.[160] It will be marked by ecological harmony and characterized above all by a thorough-going recognition of the interdependence of all things and all people which will cause compassion to flow as never before. It will be our work and God's work; we will be co-creators in a work of transformation.[161] Its human agent will be the prophet, in whom Dabhar, the creative energy of God which is God, will awaken a consciousness of the injustice and immorality which surround us.[162] The prophetic call, however, will no longer be confined to individuals, but will come upon us all.[163] When it does, we will no longer act as individuals but come together in movements, movements for black and red and women's liberation and for gay and lesbian liberation.[164] The prophet in all of us will fall in love with creation, especially with the *anawim*, the little ones of the Bible, experiencing the depth of their pain. She (for Fox, the spirit of the prophet is necessarily feminine) will launch her creativity and moral outrage in the direction of liberation and healing and into the birthing of the New Creation.[165] In this new community the despised imagination, the divine power to birth anew, will come into its own,[166] and we shall recover the earth and our earthiness.[167] Eros, the psychic urge to join, to be in the midst, to relate, to get involved, will at last have free course.[168] Thus the second coming, described by Fox as 'an awakened human spirit' will ensure the survival of Mother Earth and her children.[169] There is no question of a new heaven and a new earth; biblical eschatology is thrown overboard.

Fox, naturally enough on the basis of his definition of Eros, uses the term also in its normal sense of sexuality. Creation spirituality needs a revival of sexual mysticism,[170] for the Cosmic Christ is present in all sexuality in all its dimensions and possibilities, both heterosexual and homosexual.[171] In all true love-making, people are temples encountering temples, 'the holy of holies receiving the holy of holies'.[172] This passage is prefaced by the observation, 'The Cosmic Christ might speak thus on the topic of sexuality.'[173] But the biblical Christ would not have spoken thus on sexual activity which the Bible specifically forbids, nor would he have spoken on sexual encounter as an experience of the transcendent as Bede Griffiths also did.

Marriage is holy and the bed undefiled (*Heb. 13:4*), but it belongs to the created order. Both Griffiths and Fox at this point would have benefited from Bonhoeffer's common sense.

There are three passages in *The Coming of the Cosmic Christ* in which Fox places on the lips of Jesus himself three charismatic type prophecies. They are to be found on pages 142, 198 and 211. None of the words attributed to him echo his teaching as recorded in the Gospels. In the first the uncreated Christ is made to speak of his Creator. In the second, he is alleged to say, besides much else, 'Expect divinity to appear and reappear as a child. Expect it in yourselves.' In the third, there is a similar exhortation for us to recognize our own divinity and to be kind to Mother Earth:

Find the creative person, the 'I am,' the divine child at play and at generativity in yourself. Give birth to yourself. . . . I too am a Creator, sometimes called the Creator. But in fact I ask you to be my companions, to share the birthing of images with me, to be my co-creators. Do not bore me by refusing. Do not scandalize me by saying I can't. Do not oppress Mother Earth and her future by refusing to create and re-create. Come, play with me. Let us create together.

All the things that Christ stressed, the summons to repentance, rebirth and discipleship, and the dependency of our eternal destiny on our relationship to him, go by default. In her review of the book in *The Times* 7 August, 1992, Dr Margaret Brierley, an authority on the New Age, suggested that Fox 'virtually channels the Christ', employing the term applied to a medium through whom a demonic spirit speaks. What is certain is that Christ himself does not speak through Fox.

It is abundantly clear that Matthew Fox belongs to the New Age, not to the Christian tradition. His idea that we are co-creators with God, not shared by the pluralists in general, and therefore appropriately considered here, is the synergism which is a key concept of the New Age. It is described by Marilyn Ferguson in her *Aquarian Conspiracy*, its manifesto. All lesser groupings are building up ever more creative and beneficial complexities, until we arrive at a holistic universe, a universe that is, where everything is absorbed in the Whole. She traces the theory back to Smuts, the South African soldier, statesman and philosopher, who brought the term 'holism' into common use.[174] Matthew Fox's Dabhar, the god within us and every separate phenomenon, is none other than the New Ager's synergism, working to the same end, the abolition of all dualisms and divisions in the One. De Chardin's view of individual monads converging at the Omega point is the same doctrine. But we are not co-creators with God; we are workers together with him (*2 Cor. 6:1*), responding to his grace as he sanctifies us and exercising the ministry of reconciliation with which in his grace he has entrusted us. The change of consciousness from the fall–redemption tradition to creation spirituality is more than the change to a global consciousness demanded by the religious pluralists. In Fox's term, borrowed by him, from the historian of science Thomas Kuhn, it is 'a paradigm shift'. The New Age movement demands from us a shift of the same dimension, which they describe by the same term.

CHAPTER V

Inter-Faith and the New Age

1 : *Inter-Faith and the New Age: Common Ground*

There is now an abundance of studies of the New Age from a Christian viewpoint, and it would take us too far from our present purpose to attempt a full survey of its beliefs and practices. There are also several writings which have shown the extent to which the churches have succumbed to its influence. But the similarity between the main tenets of the protagonists of the inter-faith movement and those of the New Age has attracted little attention. It will be a useful and salutary task to consider that similarity. The most economical way of accomplishing it will be to tabulate the leading ideas on which the inter-faith movement has been based and to indicate their presence at the heart of the New Age.

Not all the supporters of the inter-faith movement would advocate all the ideas which it has proliferated, but there are certainly those who would do so, and no complete account of it could be given if any of its major contentions were ignored.

1. The inter-faith movement denies that Christ is the only incarnation and final, complete and absolute revelation of God. If he is divine, other men have to be called divine; he was not a man of a different order, but their forerunner whose purpose was to bring them to a divine level. He was historically conditioned and only relatively a revelation of God. The possibility of incarnating God is not reserved for an élite, but open to every man. Any man, in a moment of illumination, may be awakened to the presence of God within him.

2. The death of Christ is not to be considered in juridical terms and therefore cannot be considered salvific in the sense of breaking the barrier of sin between God and man and thus renewing the fellowship between them. We can no longer say, as

in the Book of Common Prayer of the Church of England, that on the cross Christ 'made . . . (by his one oblation of himself once offered) a full, perfect, and sufficient sacrifice, oblation, and satisfaction for the sins of the whole world'.

3. The Bible is no longer the supreme authority in matters of faith. It is the jettisoning of the Bible that has led to contentions 1. and 2. Like the sacred beliefs of all religions, it is historically conditioned and relative. No one faith is adequate to embrace all that is contained in the transcendent because every faith is historically conditioned and relative. No single religion can claim to have absolute truth about God. The idea of a divinely given revelation has been discarded. No religion has more than one culture's understanding of the Absolute. Because all religions contain an understanding of the Absolute, however, they all can make a contribution to man's spiritual welfare. All are equally part of humanity's spiritual heritage, and their resources need to be pooled. They are variously regarded as a reflection of an original revelation, now lost (it will be remembered that Dr Visser't Hooft believed this theory to be the basis of syncretism) or as converging into a unity.

4. It is believed that this unity may be brought about by the exploration of the mystical element in all religions. Bede Griffiths and Thomas Merton made no distinction between the mystical experiences which came to them from the Hindu scriptures or Buddhist statues and the experiences recorded in the classic Christian mystics. Experience must be given precedence over doctrine. Mystics in all traditions have argued that conceptual knowledge of God must be abandoned if God is to be known truly. Since we have not yet discussed mysticism (and in this study we cannot do so in depth), and because mysticism is important in the New Age, we may digress here to give it a brief consideration. If an experience is beyond conceptuality, we may legitimately ask if it can yield knowledge of anything. We must heed the words of Carl Henry:

The insistence that the self is totally absorbed into the religious infinite, in an ecstatic union that transcends subject-object distinctions, would . . . seem to cancel out the mystic's ability to give a personal report of the actual state of things. For lapse of self-consciousness can only mean the surrender of any personal knowledge whatsoever.[1]

It is their mystical experiences in which the subject–object distinction between God and man disappeared which caused Griffiths and Merton to adopt Hindu monism, the belief that the all is the one. But their search for the god within is distinct from much of traditional Christian mysticism. Although the early Christian mystics synthesized biblical insights with classical or Hellenistic wisdom, many key figures of the Christian tradition – Augustine, Ambrose, Bernard of Clairvaux – emphasized scriptural authority and salvation by free grace. In modern times Theresa of Lisieux emphasized the gift of free grace in which God descends to us in order to raise us up to him. The mysticism of Griffiths and Merton, and that which Matthew Fox would have us follow, is the mysticism of the East, and as we shall discover, that of the New Age.

5. The inter-faith movement not only deifies man through the mystical discovery of the god within, it also divinizes nature and the universe. Nature has the power to forgive, and matter is evolving into spirit. This feature of its thought is accompanied by a tendency to ascribe to God the feminine gender: the earth is the divine Mother of us all. Here again we have a purely immanent God. In this creation spirituality the question of individual salvation disappears, and its possibility is even denied; the salvation of creation takes precedence over the salvation of the individual.

6. Consistently with this earth-bound world view, sex, which belongs to the created order, is seen as a vehicle through which man can make contact with the transcendent.

7. In de Chardin and Matthew Fox, the whole of the universe is seen as an interdependent, interconnected network, as though its individual components had an inherent power of connection through their belonging to the All One, without any regard to the fact that it is God's handiwork, in which the components and their connections were established by a Creator.

8. Without exception, the adherents of the inter-faith movement plead for the development of a global or planetary consciousness to correspond to the interdependence of humanity in a world which has become a global village. Such a consciousness they believe to be impossible without a rapprochement of religions by the abandonment of their claims to exclusive truth,

which in any event is impossible for men to attain in their understanding of the Absolute and Unconditional. The vision of the religious pluralists is for a greater religion still to come through their ultimate convergence.

When we turn to the New Age, we shall discover that these eight bases are inherent in its teachings.

1. Christ is not unique; he is not God in the flesh assuming the function of King, Prophet and Priest. He is rather an embodiment of a state of being, Christhood, which it is possible for all men to attain. In her autobiography, Shirley MacClaine contends that Christ 'tried to teach people that they could do the same things if they got more in touch with their spiritual selves and their own potential power'.[2] According to David Spangler, formerly of the Findhorn Community in Scotland, the most important New Age centre in the British Isles, and now based in the United States, one of the most prolific New Age writers, 'The Christ is that life, love, intelligence, energetic power which maintains creation in existence. It is within each one of us'.[3] What, according to Spangler, Christ could say, 'I am attuned, I am one with the whole' (notice the monism),[4] we can all say when we attain Christhood, which we do by mystic meditation, a topic which must be postponed until we come to New Age mysticism. Spangler robs Christ of his uniqueness as much as any of the religious pluralists. He sees him merely as 'one of a line of spiritual teachers, a line that continues today',[5] and puts him in a group that includes Buddha, Mohammed, Plotinus and Pythagoras.[6] He also describes him as a Bodhisattva, who has attained the right to enter Nirvana, and who has renounced that right for the sake of humanity.[7] He joins the adherents of the inter-faith movement in writing of the Christ who pours his 'limitless spirit' on all the people of the earth ('the light that lighteth every man', *John 1:9*) and has thus manifested himself in all the religions of the world; since the Christ is a universal spirit, no one religion can possibly contain him.[8] He leaves us in no doubt that he is not speaking of the Christ of 'the mainstream Christian traditions'; we need a 'cosmic Christ', where cosmic means 'inclusiveness' and 'openness'.[9] Christ is not a religious figure, 'but rather a cosmic principle, a spiritual presence whose quality infuses and appears in various ways in all the religions and

philosophies that uplift humanity and seek unity with spirit'.[10] If Spangler is right in declaring that a Christ present in all religions is not the Christ of mainstream Christianity, the religious pluralists have excluded themselves from mainstream Christianity; if they wish to remain within it, they need to repent of their pluralism. Spangler combines his conception of a cosmic Christ, a Christ whose consciousness embraces the whole planet, with his doctrine of the Christ within; where there is openness to the universe, 'the Christ is active and present'.[11] Jesus 'was the prototype of the expression of the reality of the Christ consciousness which is inherent in us all'.[12] A time is coming when multitudes will recognize this consciousness in themselves, when there will be a mass incarnation, which Spangler terms the second coming of Christ.[13] There can be no more effective way of disposing of the uniqueness of Christ's incarnation than to envisage a mass incarnation. Spangler here is directly following de Chardin.

2. The idea of a substitutionary atonement is as repugnant to the New Ager as to the pluralist. One New Age work, *A Course in Miracles*, asserts,

'God' does not believe in retribution [these words are attributed to Jesus]. His Mind does not create that way. He does not hold your 'evil' deeds against you. Is it likely that he would hold them against me? . . . Sacrifice is a notion totally unknown to God. It arises solely from fear, and frightened people can be vicious. Sacrificing in any way is a violation of my injunction that you should be merciful even as your Father in Heaven is merciful.[14]

According to Spangler, the crucifixion had quite a different purpose from reconciling the world to God:

This is really the true crucifixion. It was not so much hanging Jesus on the physical cross, but it was the entry of the cosmic Christ in the physical, etheric, mental, and emotional energy patterns of the planetary body itself.

From that point onwards, the Christ was no longer an educative force standing outside the planet, beckoning evolution forward. It had become a very powerful force operative within the very structure of the planet itself.[15]

In Teilhardian terms, the crucifixion constituted a decisive step in the movement towards the Omega point.

3. There is a similar attitude to the Bible in the inter-faith movement and in the New Age. It has no literal authority. While the religious pluralists discard the plain meaning of its statements which contradict their position, the New Agers tend to bolster their position by allegorizing them. The text of Scripture as such has no authority for either group. Thus Spangler interprets Jesus' saying about the man who built his house upon the sand as a man who lives ignoring this own divinity.[16] He defines the kingdom of heaven as 'the state of identification with one's true individuality, the source within, the Divine centre, that I AM THAT I AM'.[17] For Spangler the revelation for the New Age is the revelation that man is God.[18] The contention of the protagonists of the inter-faith movement that any man can become an incarnation of God is a step in the direction of the New Age, and shows how easily an ill-informed Christian could become a New Ager.

Some New Agers regard themselves as esoteric Christians. These rely not on the canonical Scripture but on the Gnostic literature, the ideas of which some canonical Scripture, notably the Johannine and Pauline writings, was written to refute. They envisage an individual Christ who will return; the second coming to them is more than the realization by an individual of the god within. Their view of the nature of the Christ who is to return varies and this topic takes us out of the field of this study. Those who want to pursue it may read *The Counterfeit Christ of the New Age Movement* by Ron Rhodes.[19] What matters is that the New Age Christ to come is not the biblical Christ who is to return as King of Kings and Lord of Lords.

4. So we proceed to examine the place of mysticism in the New Age movement. New Age mysticism, like that of the religious pluralists, is a process of introversion to discover the god within and to realize Christhood. We may begin with a definition of the Christ by another New Age writer, Benjamin Creme:

The Christ . . . is an embodiment of . . . the love aspect of God. . . . He embodies the energy which is a consciousness of the Being we call God. . . . He would rather that you didn't pray to him, but to God within you, which is also in him.[20]

New Agers sometimes describe the Christ as someone who has attained a balanced love consciousness in which the spiritual and rational consciousness are in perfect harmony. But before Western man can attain this state of being, which is Christhood, he must undergo a radical transformation of consciousness. His left-brain and rational orientation must be balanced by the development of the intuitive powers of the right brain until it is in perfect harmony with his left brain so that he has attained a perfectly balanced psyche. He can do this through the aid of various psycho-techniques such as biofeedback, but above all by looking East with the advocates of the inter-faith movement and adopting Eastern style mystical meditation. The use of *mantras*, rhythmically repeated sentences, words, syllables, phrases or sounds, in order to still the rational consciousness and allow the intuitive self to surface, is particularly effective. The process of transformation by which Christhood is attained has been carefully studied by Dirk Goertz in *Transcendental Typology, The Essence of Primal New Age Theology* (Destiny Image Publishers, Shippensburg, PA, 1990), and we follow his account. The first stage in the transformation is a stripping away of the Ego, or rational perceptions of the Self, the identical process of Thomas Merton's and Matthew Fox's 'letting go'. Typical *mantras* are OM TAT SAT, TAT, where TAT refers to the Brahman, SAT to Pure Being or I AM. Here the individual concentrates on the truth I AM THAT I AM. This *mantra* is a variation on another in common use, TAT TWAM ASI, 'Thou art That', on which Bede Griffiths laid such stress.[21] In these *mantras*, the meditator is meditating on his own deity. The aim of such meditation is to direct the individual away from his Ego into his inner intuitive Self, so that he can realize his oneness with the All. There is a Sufi meditation which goes:

> I am not the body.
> I am not the senses
> I am not the mind.
> I am not this.
> I am not that.

What am I then? What is Self?
It is in the body.
It is in everybody.
It is everywhere.
It is the All.
It is Self. I am IT, Absolute Oneness.

In the first five lines, the active, rational mind is stilled. In the sixth line, concentration on the outer Self is exchanged for a consideration of the inner Self, the existence of which is acknowledged in line seven. The eighth line recognizes the collective Self, the ninth and tenth lines acknowledge the Unity and Wholeness of the universe, or the Universal Self. The last line is a meditation on the indwelling of the Universal Self and the Cosmic Consciousness.

This path may be reversed, and the rational mind stilled by concentration on the unifying principle in the universe, but the meditation will again end with its indwelling in the individual:

> I am the divine Self.
> Immortal
> Eternal
> Radiant with spiritual light.
> I am that Self of light, that Self am I.
> The Self in me, is one with the Self in all.
> I am that Self in all; that Self am I.
> I am THAT, THAT am I.[22]

Thus the transformation brought about by meditation leads to an understanding of the Self as a Universal or Collective Self, which is part of an even greater Universal Self or Cosmic Consciousness. This Cosmic Consciousness is the ultimate power in the universe, not working on it from without, but inherent in every material and immaterial object or phenomenon within it. There is then no longer an experiencing subject or experienced object, the dualism so frowned on by Matthew Fox, and we are back with Hinduism monism, the version of Hinduism preferred by Bede Griffiths and Thomas Merton. The entry into this understanding of the Self (Myself, the Universal Self, the Cosmic Self) cannot be expressed in rational or cognitive terms, because in New Age mysticism, as we have seen in the case of inter-faith mysticism to which it so closely approximates, there is no longer a knowing subject and nothing to know; with the abandonment of dualism both disappear. Marilyn Ferguson's *The Aquarian Conspiracy* describes it as a 'spontaneous, mystical or psychic experience as hard to explain as it is to deny'.[23] Nevertheless it is an experience which is referred to as the attainment of Christhood, and also as the *birthing* or second coming of Christ, and confers on those so transformed the consciousness that they transcend the material and rational worlds and possess within themselves the elements of the eternal, immaterial world, that is, the attributes of divinity.

The mysticism of the inter-faith movement and of the New Age has the same root and the same result; it is a movement of introversion which leads to the Self enjoying itself in the ecstasy of its altered consciousness. It is interesting that the advocates of contemplative prayer regularly recommended the use of a *mantra* as a starting-point. The question arises whether this type of meditation leads to a different experience from the ecstasy into which Tennyson fell by the continued repetition of his own name, or from the transformed consciousness which the New Age seeks. The use of a *mantra* inevitably stills the conscious mind and allows the mystical side of our nature free play, but it does not bring us into contact with the transcendent. That most sagacious of divines, Jonathan Edwards, reminded us that the 'saints are "taken" with "the beauty of God", other religionists with "the beauty of their experiences of God"'. But in modern spirituality, the experience which the mystics enjoy is an experience which dissolves all distinctions, especially the distinction between the perceiver and the object of his perception, into a single, undifferentiated unity. The interpretation of this experience leads directly to the presupposition of monistic philosophy, that there is only one Reality. From this it follows that all objects and individuals are emanations of the all-inclusive One. This ultimate Reality is often identified with Pure Consciousness in the sense of unlimited and unconditional awareness, in Hindu terms Sat-Cit-Ananda, Being-Awareness-Bliss, the ecstasy of consciousness aware of itself. Instead of meditating on the revealed inscripturated truths about God, which he has commanded us to do, the individual sinks into the void of letting go.

Both the inter-faith movement and the New Age movement have proved the accuracy of Nels Ferré's assessment of the theological scene made as far back as 1961:

The main fight, make no mistake, is between the Christian faith in its inner classical meaning and the new Orientalized versions whether they come via Neoplatonism or in modern forms. . . . The supernaturalistic, personalistic, classical Christian faith is now being undermined by an ultimately non-dualistic, impersonal or transpersonal faith. The winds are blowing gale-strong out of the Orient.[24]

5. The New Age movement is at one with the inter-faith movement in deifying the earth and the universe, for example in the ICOREC liturgies and the Assisi celebration of the World Wide Fund, as the World Wildlife Fund is now known. This aspect of the New Age is closely linked with its adoption of the feminist cause (also espoused by the religious pluralists), because it generally sees the earth as a goddess. Here the New Age adds a spiritual dimension to James Lovelock's well-known Gaia hypothesis that the earth is a self-sustaining organism which will destroy man if man does not stop endangering it. Lovelock's hypothesis, though he argues for its secularity, seems to have come to him through a mystical experience. In Brent Tor in the West Country, he found a place where God and Gaia met, a place for worship.[25] Typical of the New Age attitude to the earth is the Sierra Club's source book, *Well Body, Well Earth* (Sierra Club Books, San Francisco, 1983), which tells us how to make contact with the spirit of Mother Earth:

You are now in a deeply relaxed state, and level of consciousness at which your mind feels peaceful and open. At this level you can be in touch with those forces in the universe that stabilize systems and encourage health and well-being. You can now experience the visualizations vividly and pleasantly . . .

When you are done with your conversation with the spirit of the living Earth, say goodbye to it, just as you would say goodbye upon parting from a friend . . . The more you contact the voice of the living Earth, and evaluate what it says, the easier it will become for you to contact it and trust what it provides.[26]

This could well have been penned by Matthew Fox. The deification of man in the thesis that any man can incarnate God and the deification of nature and the earth go hand in hand. In his study, *Unmasking the New Age*, D. R. Groothuis tells how on one university campus he was handed a pamphlet which included a passage containing the quintessence of New Age spirituality:

I am a pagan and I dedicate myself to channelling the Spiritual Energy of my Inner Self to help and to heal myself and others.

I know that I am a part of the Whole of Nature. May I grow in my understanding of the Unity of all Nature. . . . May I always be mindful that I create my own reality and that I have the power within me to create positivity in my life.

May I always be mindful that the Goddess and God in all their forms dwell within me and that this divinity is reflected through my own inner Self, my Pagan Spirit.[27]

Although there are New Agers who believe they are rescuing Christianity from centuries of male-imposed dogma and have recovered its truth by mystical interpretations of the Bible and offer us an esoteric Christianity which will be recognized as its genuine essence by those who have undergone the obligatory transformation, many openly call themselves pagan and with paganism embrace the goddess. Equally opposed to patriarchalism, they have turned to pre-Christian nature worship in which goddesses play so large a part. In common with Matthew Fox, they wish to replace the worship of a Father God and the male dominance which they argue exploited nature as well as womanhood and squeezed the planet dry of resources by the more compassionate culture, as they see it, of the ancient Mother Goddess. They are so imbued with ecological concerns that the term ecofeminism has been coined to describe the movement they represent. From the beginning, the goddess in all her manifestations, whether as Ishtar in Babylon, Astarte in Canaan, Artemis in Greece, or Frigga in early Norway, has been associated with fertility and the earth. 'The Greeks', says Christian R. Downing, 'called this Goddess of the beginning Gaia, which means earth'.[28] Accordingly 'ecofeminism develops the connections between ecology and feminism that social ecology needs in order to reveal its own avowed goal of creating a free and ecological way of life'.[29] Adherents of the goddess look forward to a world without authority figures or male saviours in which we will all benefit from the saving and sustaining power of nature.

The return to the goddess is also manifested in the revival of Wicca or witchcraft. By presenting Wicca as a natural spirituality of ecological wholeness, it is hoped that it will lose its association with the demonic form which it suffered during the period when men dominated religion. One of its most prominent leaders, Starhawk, whom we have met as a colleague of Matthew Fox,[30] declares that the 'model of the Goddess . . . fosters respect for the sacredness of all living things.' Witchcraft can be seen as a religion of ecology. Its goal is harmony with nature, so that life may not just survive, but thrive.[31] Practitioners of Wicca come together in covens to 'practise the craft', as witchcraft is euphemistically termed and kindle the goddess within. Again, we may cite Starhawk:

The Goddess . . . is the world. Manifest in each of us. She can be known by every individual, in all her magnificent diversity. . . . Religion is a matter of relinking with the divine within and with her outer manifestations in all of the human and natural world.[32]

Once more we meet with the One All and the All One. The monistic nature of magic and its belief in the interconnectedness of all things is stressed by Starhawk in an explanation of its rituals:

The primary principle of magic is connection. The universe is a fluid, ever-changing energy pattern, not a collection of fixed and separate things. What affects one thing affects, in some way, all things: all is interwoven into the continuous fabric of being, its warp and weft and energy, which is the essence of magic.[33]

The names of the goddess are many, but the identity of the goddess is one. One feminist writer takes male writers to task for breaking the goddess figure down into unnumerable goddesses, when every 'female divinity . . . may be regarded as only another aspect of the core concept of a female Supreme Being'.[34] Ultimately, the goddess cult is only another form taken by the concept of the All One and the One All. Quoting from a witch's study of Neopaganism which analyzes its basic tenet as a 'Thou

Art God/dess' concept, and that we are to become what we are potentially, Groothuis concludes,

The pantheon of gods and goddesses are but symbolic representations of the One reality, the totality of Nature. Divinity is sought within the self – which is really nothing but the cosmic Self (the One) in disguise.[35]

In dealing with the pluralists earlier we noticed but did not comment on their ascription of the feminine gender to God. Since we have now come across the same usage in the New Age, we may pause briefly to discuss the biblical usage. We may begin with Carl Henry's analysis:

In sharp distinction from the Near Eastern fertility cults and their nature gods, the Bible studiously avoids imputing sexual organs to God even anthropomorphically [Bede Griffiths take note!]. Feminine and masculine sexual elements are excluded from both the Old and New Testament doctrine of deity. The God of the Bible is a sexless God. When Scripture speaks of God as 'he' the pronoun is primarily personal (generic) rather than masculine (specific); it emphasizes God's personality . . . in contrast to impersonal entities.[36]

The charge that the language of the Bible is sexist is baseless. The Bible values highly both women and men, and does not avoid feminine images for God. Jesus speaks of himself as a hen which gathers her chickens under its wings (*Matt. 23:37*), and God is said to have given birth to Israel (*Deut. 32:18*), to cry like a travailing mother (*Isa. 42:14*), and to have more than a mother's care for his children (*Isa. 49:15*). But God is never referred to as 'she' or described as feminine. Jesus taught his disciples to pray 'Our Father'. Susan Foh says, 'For the fatherhood and motherhood to be significant, there must be a difference between fatherhood and motherhood'.[37] Mothers and fathers share personhood, but have different functions in parenting. If the Bible is inspired by God, we should not dispense with its imagery. C. S. Lewis has reminded us that God himself has taught us how to speak of him. God is personal, while in the goddess religions the goddess is not a person at all, but a personification of the One, the impersonal matrix or principle of existence, 'the maternal ground of being'.[38]

The deification of the earth leads New Agers naturally into a deep appreciation of the indigenous peoples who live most closely in contact with it. Thomas Berry, a nature theologian, writes:

What we need . . . is the sensitivity to understand and respond to the psychic energies deep in the very structure of reality itself . . . This is the ultimate wisdom of tribal peoples.[39]

Nowhere is this more apparent than in the little publicized World Wilderness Congress, the brain child of Zulu chief Magqubu Ntombela and fostered by Ian Playfair, a friend of Sir Laurens van der Post who considered Ntombela to be a repository of all the wisdom which indigenous peoples have to offer us. Some of its reports have been published by the Findhorn Community, which hosted its third congress, in reporting which the Congress described itself as without formal doctrine or creed, but as 'based on the idea that humanity is involved in an evolutionary expansion of consciousness which will, in term, create new patterns of civilization and promote a planetary culture infused with spiritual values'.[40] We have by now discovered what the New Age spiritual values are. Sir Laurens van der Post is a prominent member of the Wilderness Congress. Addressing its second meeting, held at Cairns, Australia, in 1980, he describes how after the Second World War he found himself unable to rejoin society until he had regathered spiritual strength by a period of retirement in the bush. Before this ended, there was a thunderstorm which brought the rain so badly needed by the earth. It so refreshed him and gave him an impulse to pray, not the Lord's prayer, which he felt inadequate for the occasion. Instead he found himself praying, 'Our Mother which art in earth, may thy love be fulfilled, so that will and love become one'.[41] His address was entitled 'Wilderness and the Human Spirit' and its theme was how humanity had lost its sense of belonging. He referred to St. Paul's promise that one day we would know as we are known (*1 Cor. 13:12*), words which he believed came from the wilderness within him. He did not understand that Paul was speaking out of his experience of God. When he spoke of humanity's feeling of lostness, van der Post was not thinking of the rupture between man and God, but of the breach between man and nature. Man would recover the kingdom of heaven by following the advice of a passage he quoted froe Dead Sea Scrolls:

Follow the birds, the beasts and the fish, and they will lead you in.

'And that', he concluded, 'really is what those of us who believe in wilderness try to ensure and to do. It is all we believe, and we can take the answer and carry it as a banner with what we are trying to do'.[42] The theme again is the interdependence of all things, especially the interdependence of man and the earth. By exploiting the outer wilderness of nature, we have cut ourselves off from our inner wilderness, 'the garden world within our own spirit'.[43] At the third World Wilderness Congress, Sir Laurens van der Post spoke of the privilege he had of living for three and a half years in close contact with the bushmen of the Kalahari desert and the tragedy of the destruction of wilderness man:

In a way that is the greatest loss of all because this person could have been our real bridge to knowing wilderness and nature in the way in which it is known by the creator and in which it should really be known.[44]

We must not be misled, however, by the word 'creator'. At the Fourth World Wilderness Congress at Denver, another New Age centre, in 1987, a Canadian Indian, Norma Kassi, referred in her address to a saying of a chief of her race about the natural and spiritual law which we must obey or perish. She commented:

These are wise words, spoken by one representing a people . . . who have been more closely connected with the Earth Mother than most of us, and who have lived in an awareness of the Great Spirit . . . the leaf emblem of the Wilderness Congress represents this wisdom . . . The two smaller leaves lower down on the stem represent man's relationship with man and man's relationship with the earth. But the central frond . . . represents man's relationship with God. This isn't the God of common and religious belief, but one who simply represents the way life works: a symbol of the universal law, the universal spirit which informs us all.[45]

There could be no clearer illustration of the fundamentally impersonal nature of the New Age god.

One of the best known environmental organizations is Greenpeace, which also draws its ideology from an indigenous culture, that of the American Indians. It has published a pamphlet explaining that it believes that when the earth is sick and animal life has ceased, a tribe drawn from all creeds, races and cultures will come to restore the earth to its former beauty. This tribe will be called Warriors of the Rainbow. Hence they have taken the rainbow as their symbol, which is also the symbol of the New Age in general. It is sometimes called an 'International Sign of Peace'. In origin it is occult. It represents a bridge between the individual and the Universal Mind, which in the branch of the New Age which regards itself as esoteric Christianity is referred to as Sanat Kumara, one of its terms for Lucifer. In this context the rainbow is termed the Antahkaranah. According to David Spangler, formerly of the Findhorn community, as already mentioned, Christians have a distorted view of Lucifer in treating him as the enemy of God and man. He writes,

It is important to see that Lucifer, as I am using this term, describes an angel, a being, a great and mighty planetary consciousness. It does not describe that popular thought-form of Satan who seeks to lead man down a path of sin and wrongdoing. That is a human creation, and yet it is a creation that has some validity but represents the collective thought-form of all those negative energies which man has built up and created.

Man is his own Satan just as man is his own salvation. But since the energies of Lucifer go to build up this thought-form, Lucifer, or shall I say a shadow Lucifer, can be identified with this thought-form, and in this there is confusion. If one can approach this thought-form with love, without fear, then one can go beyond this shadow and see the true angel of light that is there seeking to bring light to man's inner world.

Of course, yes, the forces of evil are part of God. They are not separate from God. Everything is God.[46]

Like the New Age, the World Council of Churches in its Vancouver and Canberra Assemblies reached out beyond the Eastern religions to embrace indigenous cultures.[47] This throws some light on its own reference to the rainbow in the document issued at Vancouver, 'Between the Flood and the Rainbow: Covenanting for Justice, Peace and the Integrity of Creation'.

One New Age book is entitled *The New Rainbow Serpent, and Justice, Peace and Integrity of Creation.* In many cultures the rainbow is closely associated with the serpent. This is particularly true of the rainbow-hued snakes of Australian and West African mythologies. It will be remembered, too, that ICOREC chose a rainbow-coloured thread to symbolize its covenant with creation and the life it contained.[48] It may be that the W.C.C. and ICOREC had the Noachic covenant mainly in mind. The title of the Vancouver document, however, so closely resembles the title of the New Age book just mentioned that one wonders if some New Age influence was behind it. Similarly, as echo of the New Age is discernible in ICOREC's choice of the rainbow as a symbol for its covenant with creation. The tying of the rainbow-coloured threads was based on the similar procedure followed at the World Wide Fund's Assisi celebration, which was explained as a borrowing from Hinduism,[49] where in Yoga, the Kundalini, the fiery serpent power within the body, plays a key role; its arousal is supposed to result in enlightenment.

6. The New Age supports the protagonists of the inter-faith movement in believing that sex can be a vehicle for experiencing the transcendent. Bede Griffiths accepted this Hindu belief without reservation, and also saw sacredness in the Canaanite fertility cults, which were an abomination in the sight of God (*1 Kings 11:5, 7*). The New Age attitude to sex varies. Some of its activists recommend multifarious erotic relationships, others advocate total abstinence. But the aim of both groups is the same, the attainment of ultimate wholeness through a transformed consciousness. Eastern mysticism holds that two opposite but interconnected principles permeate the cosmos, *yin* and *yang*, the male and the female. The two have different characteristics: the *yin* principle is dark, receptive, immaterial, organic and intuitive, the *yang* principle is clear, rational, complex, strong and creative. *Yin* and *yang* are inherent in everything in the universe, and their union, material or immaterial, leads to divine wholeness. Sexual union is itself divine. For New Agers, sexual intercourse is a potential means of experiencing the transcendental consciousness of the fully transformed individual, for whom sex will be an experience of the unity of the cosmos. Yoga is recommended by most advocates

of the inter-faith movement. One form of yoga, *karezza*, is meditation combined with prolonged intercourse without orgasm with the sole purpose of attaining spiritual illumination in a higher state of consciousness. Sexual union thus becomes a form of worship. The male and female principles unite and opposites are transcended. Both partners are expected to meditate more deeply on the oneness of the cosmos. Besides *karezza*, which limits the altered consciousness to the duration of the sexual union, sexual abstinence is valued because the energy required by the sexual act is released to be used in meditation. For men, the conservation of the sexual fluid is considered valuable because it is held to be a form of psychic power, which, when retained, heightens the intuitive consciousness. Abstinence is indeed considered to be the ultimate form of oneness with the cosmos. In a fully evolved humanity, sexual union will be unnecessary to propagate the human race, because it will have transcended the need for material bodies. The transcendence of the physical will result in an androgynous humanity that will be one with the I AM. In the meantime, anything goes, because all human beings as parts of the interconnected universe are parts of each other. Matthew Fox's erotic celebration can have free play.

7. The New Age adopts the same view of an interconnected and interdependent universe found in the inter-faith movement. The monism which imbues it because of its taking on board Eastern mysticism and which runs like a thread through the inter-faith movement is paradoxically presented for acceptance to the West on the rationalistic ground that it is required by the findings of modern science. The mechanistic view of Newtonian science with its clockwork picture of nature working in fixed and predictable patterns determined by inviolable laws has been overthrown by Einstein's theory of relativity and Heisenberg's indeterminacy principle. Matter and energy are no longer distinct phenomena but interchangeable: matter absorbs heat energy and emits light energy in unexpected lumps or sparks which Einstein called quanta and are now called photons. Light can be described both as waves and particles; neither excludes the other. The old conception of hard mechanical matter has been discarded; matter is no longer reducible to

neat divisible pieces that obey mathematical rules. The physicist Fritjof Capra describes the present view:

Subatomic particles are not 'things' but are interconnections between 'things' and these 'things', in turn, are interconnections between other 'things', and so on. In quantum theory you never end up with 'things'; you always deal with interconnections.[50]

The significance of Capra for our study is that he has embraced all the varied causes championed by the New Age – holistic health, environmentalism, global politics and the one universal consciousness; he is the New Ager *par excellence*. He has himself experienced the heightened stage of consciousness which is the point of entry into the New Age. It came to him through a mystical experience:

Five years ago, I had a beautiful experience. . . . I was sitting by the ocean one late summer afternoon, watching the waves roll in and feeling the rhythm of my breathing, when I became aware of my whole environment as being engaged in a great cosmic dance. Being a physicist, I knew that the sand, rocks, water and air around me were made of vibrating molecules and atoms . . . but until that moment I had only experienced it through graphs, diagrams and mathematical theories. As I sat on that beach my former experiences came to life; I 'saw' cascades of energy coming down from outer space, in which particles were created and destroyed in rhythmic pulses; I 'saw' the atoms of the elements and those of my body participating in this cosmic dance of energy; I felt its rhythm and I 'heard' its sound, and at that moment I *knew* that this was the dance of Shiva, the Lord of the Dancers worshipped by the Hindus.[51]

The result of this experience was the writing of his influential book, *The Tao of Physics*, in which by juxtaposing the statements of physicists and passages from Buddhist, Tao and Hindu mystics (e.g. pp. 149–155, ibid.), he set out to establish the oneness of all things:

The picture of an interconnected cosmic web which emerges from modern physics has been used extensively in the East to convey the mystical experience of nature. For the Hindus, *Brahman* is the unifying thread in the cosmic web, the ultimate ground of all being:

> He on whom the sky, the earth and the atmosphere
> Are woven, and the wind, together with all-life breaths,
> Him alone know as the one Soul [Mundaka Upanishad].[52]

In a later book, *The Turning Point*, he describes the ultimate state of consciousness as one 'in which all boundaries and dualisms have been transcended and all individuality dissolves into universal, undifferentiated oneness'.[53] There are not many selves but one Self, the One; TAT TWAM ASI.[54] His mistake is to identify the biblical model of creation with the deistic one – God turned on the machine, and left it to run by itself. But God is not a clockmaker removed from creation, which was created and is unified by Christ, the Logos, the Word of God. Interestingly, he acknowledges that he has adopted many scientific theories which would not be commonly accepted because of his personal beliefs and allegiances.[55] In Capra, we have a personal link between the New Age movement and the inter-faith movement. He was one of the many visitors to Bede Griffiths' ashram. Conversely, Bede Griffiths supported his religious position in one of his last books, *A New Vision of Reality* (Collins, 1989), by using Capra's picture of the new physics.

Capra had a forerunner in his view of the interdependence of all things in Teilhard de Chardin who is regarded by the New Age as one of its founding fathers. Marilyn Ferguson's *Aquarian Conspiracy* mentions his name fifteen times in its index. In de Chardin we thus have another link between the New Age movement and the inter-faith movement. The author of another New Age book, *New Genesis, Shaping a Global Spirituality*,[56] Robert Muller, Secretary of the UN's Economic and Social Council, a Roman Catholic, speaks of his 'Teilhardian enlightenments'.[57] The first was being taught by him to think universally and embrace 'every aspect of our planetary home'.[58] The second was the impact on him of de Chardin's vision of a global evolution which would culminate in 'the birth of a collective brain to the human species'.[59] The third was the inspiration which he received from de Chardin's 'vision of the earth as a "living cell"' and 'his outcry for responsible earth management'.[60] The fourth was his discovery of 'the "natural", "evolutionary", "divine", "universal" or "cosmic" laws which must rule our journey in the cosmos',[61] which he terms 'the spiritual transcendence' which de Chardin saw as 'the next step in our evolution'.[62] The fifth and last came from de Chardin's ability to infer the whole universe from a single flower or insect,[63] yet one more illustration of the belief in the All-One. It is in keeping with New Age thought and with the inter-faith movement and their belief in the interconnectedness of all things that he should extol the god within:

I could focus my attention and love from a flower or a person to the universe and God, from the infinite past to the infinite future; I could profit from the incredible expansion of my hands, arms, legs, eyes, ears, and brain through technology: *I could seek, know and feel in myself the entire universe and Godhead, for I was part of them and they were part of me . . . and last but not least I was the master of my cosmos.*[64]

Muller experienced the change of consciousness, the point of entry into the New Age, through reading the mystics.[65] He was also a student of Thomas Merton and a participant in East–West monastic encounter.[66] He saw it as the duty of religions to 'accelerate their ecumenism and create common world religious institutions which would bring the resources and inspirations of the religions to bear upon the solution of world problems'.[67]

8. This last observation brings us to the final point where the New Age and the inter-faith movement stand on common ground, their globalism. In the latter, this theme runs without intermission from Sir Francis Younghusband to Matthew Fox. In 1972, Donald Keys, a consultant to United Nations delegations and committees, founded an association entitled Planetary Citizens. His aim was through political action

to orchestrate . . . a general awakening, a crossing of the threshold to global awareness . . . for as large a part of the population of the world as we can. . . . There has to be some critical mass of public awareness, of planetary consciousness, before politicians will move, before foreign offices will get into gear, before teaching changes in the schools.[68]

Keys believes humanity is 'on the verge of something entirely new, a further evolutionary step unlike any other in the emergence of the first global civilization'.[69] We are approaching de Chardin's Omega point, the unification of consciousness and culture. In 1982, Planetary Citizens and other groups launched a consciousness raising project which they called 'Planetary Initiative for the World We Choose', which led to a Planetary Congress in 1983 attended by five hundred people, including a galaxy of New Age luminaries. This issued a declaration published in the periodical of Planetary Citizens, 'The Initiator', which stated that pivotal to 'a fulfilling and harmonious future' was the need to achieve 'the individual human potential and . . . the essential spiritual identity of each person, *giving rise to a oneness with all life*'.[70] In similar vein, Greenpeace affirms that 'our ultimate goal . . . is to help bring about that basic change in thinking known as "planetary consciousness"'.[71] Another political group, World Goodwill, shares the goals of Planetary Citizens. The headquarters of both are situated in the United Nations Plaza.

2: *Martin Palmer: the New Age Enters the Church*

With so much common ground between them, it is not surprising that supporters of the inter-faith movement have provided a platform for the New Age movement. Starhawk has expressed her delight at the response she has received from the churches through the position given her by Matthew Fox in his Institute for Culture and Creation Spirituality:

Teaching ritual and the history of the Goddess religion to priests, nuns and Christian educators was a new experience but deeply rewarding. I found the students very open to new ideas, hungry for new forms of ritual and very creative. . . . *I am very glad to discover such a strong movement within Christian churches that is sympathetic to the Pagan Spirit and willing to learn from the teachings of the Old Religion.*[72]

The readiness of Christendom to learn from Starhawk's 'old religion' is not just a transatlantic phenomenon. From 30 September to 3 October, 1994, Anglicans and Roman Catholics met with pagans, druids and witches near Avebury, Wiltshire. These three non-Christian groups have much in common. The last is most widespread, and we need only consider its religion, Wicca. According to one of its recent expositors, a psychiatrist attracted to it by her study of Jung, it rejects the belief in one true God in comparison with whom all others are false. It also repudiates all religions founded on revelation, which it argues imposes on them a rigidity which prevents them playing a useful role in evolution. What is to be revered is the life force. We need to remember that we are now in the age of Aquarius, the New Age, when the divine god and goddess will be found in every man and woman, 'not just in one perfect man now dead'. This godhead within is to be found by consciousness-raising techniques. Wicca sees the circle as a place of healing and refuge, and therefore emphasizes the importance of circular dancing, which allows individual personalities to merge into a group entity, achieves the aim of heightening the consciousness, and, above all, by releasing etheric energy, brings the physical world into contact with psychic forces, uniting the material world with what it conceives as the spiritual. The Avebury meeting included a circle dance in its activities. Those who claimed the name of Christian thus participated in a solemn rite with those who repudiated everything which makes Christianity Christian – the one true God, and sinless Christ and a divine revelation. A Roman Catholic priest who addressed the gathering is reported in the *Church Times* of 7 October as saying, 'in the end there is only the one experience, "I am Who I Am", though we don't all experience it in the same way'. But the self-existent divine 'I AM THAT I AM' of Exodus 3:14 cannot be the god within of Wicca, and to approximate the two is syncretism, in which Christianity is abandoned.

The same willingness to embrace the New Age is found in St. James' Church, Piccadilly, whose affiliations with the New Age are well known. Here we may give one example. During the weekend of 15 May, 1994, it held a conference addressed by Eileen Caddy of the Findhorn Community. The communion service on the Sunday began with the chanting of the Hindu OM. It was led by the curate, a radical feminist, and all male references to God in the liturgy were changed, except for the retention of 'Father' in the Lord's Prayer. The creed was omitted. The preacher was a priestess of the Order of Isis. She explained that her aim was 'to create values which transcend all religions' and urged the congregation to let the divine spirit, which she experienced as female as well as male, to 'live and move in them'. She spoke of God as 'It' and of the Trinity as myth and metaphor. Before the Thanksgiving Prayer, members of the congregation were invited to join hands and give each other a 'magic squeeze'. After this they were invited to join 'a most ancient form of meditative dance'. When the rector, the Rev Donald Reeves, broke the bread he held it out in four directions with the explanation that he was doing so for all the ancient religious tradition, Buddhism, Hinduism, Islam and

Judaism, 'that one day we may be one'. After the close of the service he told the congregation how the New Age had enlightened him, and applauded the leaders of the 'Alternatives' (the New Age programme) at St. James. Finally, he described how he had led the pre-ordination retreat for the first women to be ordained in Hereford Cathedral. On the Saturday night, they locked themselves in the cathedral, where they laid their hands on the pillars and performed other rituals. The women, so long rejected by the church, made their peace with it by stroking the effigies of dead bishops in the building. They sat on the communion table, claiming the cathedral for themselves. Lastly, to express their joy at being ordained, they performed a circle dance, with the Bishop of Hereford participating. They may have been ignorant of the meaning of the circle dance in Wicca but it is significant that the spiritual power which it is intended to raise includes 'woman spirit'.[73] What happened at Hereford on this occasion is as pagan as the meeting at Avebury.

With Matthew Fox and the ICOREC liturgies the New Age has entered the churches. Of more relevance to us in England is Martin Palmer, whose activities and influence in the Anglican Church extend far beyond his inter-faith liturgies which have been celebrated in its cathedrals. One of his most recent books, *Living Christianity*, comes with an episcopal endorsement. His word has earned him the reputation of being a New Ager, even a New Age guru, a charge he has attempted to repudiate in his *Coming of Age, an Exploration of Christianity and the New Age* (Aquarian/Thorson, London, 1993). There he takes to task some critics of the New Age for regarding it as a monolithic and conspiratorial movement. He has some justification for his rejection of the first adjective, because the New Age embraces a multitude of diverse views and practices, and perhaps also for his denial of the second. But many New Agers regard themselves as conspirators; the New Age is the 'Aquarian Conspiracy' in which countless 'networks' worldwide, each concentrating on one activity, are working together to produce the evolutionary quantum leap which they believe is the next stage in the development of humanity. It describes its method as 'networking'. The networking, however, may be too loose and uncoordinated to merit the status of a full-blown conspiracy. These, however, are minor matters. The New Age, in all its diversity, has two beliefs, the One All and All One, and its corollary, the god within each individual. Palmer progesses to repudiate the first. In another book, *Living Christianity* (Element, Shaftesbury, Dorset, 1993), he writes, 'I do believe that there is a purposeful God behind, within and through creation'.[74] Nevertheless in the same work he looks longingly at the monism of the East: 'Hinduism and Taoism taught that the One was to be found in the many and the many in the One'.[75] Christianity with its Creator/creature dichotomy separates nature from the divine, thus desanctifying it, and enabling 'for better or for worse' the development of modern science.[76] He also describes the view that nature is separate from God as a myth we accept uncritically which needs to be re-examined. He is clearly not completely happy with the belief that there is a God behind nature. The second basic tenet of the New Age, the God within, he views favourably, regarding it as a corollary of the foundational Christian doctrine of the incarnation:

Much of Christian and Jewish mysticism is concerned with the individual engagement with the God potential within us, or of our potentialities once we allow God within us. That it has not been commonly perceived as being part of the Christian tradition has to do with the constant emphasis on the remoteness and authority of God rather than on the indwelling nature of the idea of incarnation. Christianity, of all faiths, should be able to handle in a mature way the concept of both a God without and the divine within . . . In our own age, few people have been aware that this tradition of the 'God within' is to be found in Orthodoxy, Catholicism, Methodism, and in fact is fundamental to Christian incarnational thought.[77]

Self-development and self-awareness and a response to something greater than the self are common, according to Palmer, both to Christianity and the New Age.[78]

Before examining Palmer's thought more closely, we must pause to take account of the introductory biographical preface to *Coming of Age*. There he describes how in his youth he walked on the Marlborough Downs with elderly men following ley lines, watched middle-aged women telling fortunes and reading crystal balls,[79] and haunted the second-hand bookshops of Bristol, where he liked to search the occult section containing piles of the writings of Madame Blavatsky and the 1934 Year Book of the Society for Psychical Research, where he found 'gems' on a variety of occult topics which fascinated him.[80] Thus he had from early years an unhealthy interest in the occult and his gems have nullified his power of spiritual discernment in the same way in which Dom Bede Griffiths was affected by listening to the theosophical readings to which he was subjected at the same stage of life.[81]

One of the aspects of the New Age about which Palmer has a good deal to say is channelling, which we mentioned briefly in connection with Matthew Fox.[82] Many New Agers believe they are channels for messages they receive passively from an Ascended Master or some lesser being they believe to be active in bringing humanity to a higher stage in the evolution which is leading us to a collective consciousness. Palmer rightly tells us that channelling is not a new phenomenon but as old as religion itself. It is found in Taoism and the Qur'an is an instance of it. Very commonly the words reported by the channellers are heard in a state of ecstasy or trance. On this basis, Palmer regards channelling as identical with Old Testament prophecy, though he differentiates between the value of the content of Old Testament prophecy and that of the modern channeller.[83] The prophets of the Old Testament dealt with the relationship of God and his chosen people, while most contemporary channellers are concerned with individual issues and wishes for happiness. But the recorded prophecies of the Old Testament contain only a little of the sum total of the prophecy given in the Old Testament period, and if we had a record of it we would find it as banal and irrelevant as the outpourings of modern channellers.[84] The recorded prophecy of the Old Testament represented a peak, but is not therefore to be regarded as a different phenomenon from channelling today. Rejecting the idea of a personal devil, Palmer cannot recognize the demonic character of channelling and does not regard it as dangerous in itself, and even if channellers are merely projecting their own ideas through a supposed spirit, it is not to be dismissed out of hand.[85] The test for evaluating the messages which emerge from channelling is not their source, divine or human (Palmer's presuppositions prevent him from considering the possibility of a demonic element), but their content:

The question arises – how can you tell the 'genuine' and 'important' from the fraudulent or peripheral? I suppose one criterion is, does the message have a consistency or pose a challenge?

In other words, beware of comforting messages which tell you what you want to hear. Pay attention to radical critiques, challenges to self-satisfaction and to the status quo. The more uncomfortable the message is, the more significant it is likely to be.[86]

Palmer is unaware that Satan can be challenging as well as comforting if it suits his purposes, just as God will rebuke or encourage his people according to the need of the moment. If Palmer were aware of Satan, it would be blasphemy to classify Isaiah and Alice Bailey, for example, as demonstrating the same phenomenon. He knows nothing, in theory or in practice, of the biblical injunction to test the spirits (*1 John 4:1*).

It is not surprising therefore that he tells us that his god speaks to him through the Chinese 'I Ching', which he describes as 'the oldest divination book in the world',[87] which shows how to receive guidance through chance, 'through the totally random method for selecting a hexagram and line',[88] which means abandoning reason and logic, as the New Agers wish us to do, even if their favoured method of being guided by intuition is apparently not advised by the 'I Ching', which nevertheless

allows us to touch briefly the underlying flow of life, call this God, the divine or even the flow of nature – the name is irrelevant'.[89]

Language of this looseness allows us to ask whether Palmer truly believes in a God behind nature, or whether his mind is fixed on the One All and the All One, and his creed the monism of the New Age. In any event the god who speaks to him through the 'I Ching',[90] cannot be the God and Father of our Lord Jesus Christ, who expressly forbids all forms of divination (*Deut. 18:14*).

In spite of his claim to believe in a God behind nature, Palmer evinces in more than one place in his writings the pull that monism has over him. He notes that the New Age combines monism and progressive evolution in an alliance that cannot happily co-exist.[91] In this he is wrong. He forgets that in de Chardin's evolutionary scheme, the All are progressively moving to union with the One, and that the One is drawing the All into absorption with itself at the Omega point.[92] Monism and progressive evolution thus cohere in a perfectly logical system. We found the same to be true in Sri Aurobindo.[93] In this context Palmer asserts that monism is more intellectually and spiritually challenging than progressive evolution, because it leaves room for the concept of the fall of man, which progressive evolution does not. He is wrong again. He is not of course referring to the biblical fall, but to the fall as the division between the individual and the All[94] which is precisely de Chardin's view of the fall.[95]

His attraction to monism is also shown in his approval of Fritjof Capra, who by his illustration of the parallels between modern physicists and Eastern mystics has made possible 'a renewed way of understanding and of relating to ourselves which is not only rooted and knowledgeable, but also innovating and challenging'.[96]

If it is true, as we have suggested, that whenever the term 'goddess' is used, we have to do with the cosmic self (the One) in disguise, then Palmer's scarcely qualified acceptance of the New Age advocacy of the goddess tradition is also evidence of the monistic trend of his thought:

Once the Goddess ruled and . . . with her eclipse we lost touch with the vital nurturing aspect of the divine, with nature itself, still so often styled Mother Nature. . . . This is a case which I think has a lot to commend it, even if it is often stated with the absoluteness reserved for patriarchy.[91]

What is certain, as in the ICOREC harvest liturgy, is that nature is equated with the divine.

One thing Palmer shares with the New Age is a thorough-going hatred of biblical Christianity. According to David Spangler, Lucifer is 'the angel of man's inner evolution' who has a positive role, along with 'the Christ' in advancing humanity's cosmic consciousness.[98] Biblical Christians are at a low stage of evolution, and unfit to lead the planet to the New Age; 'it is obvious that in conducting the affairs of a spiritual society, one would not turn to those less attuned'.[99] Reiterated in Spangler's writings is the threat that those who refuse to accept 'the Christ' will be sent to a dimension other than physical embodiment, in which their needed evolution will be advanced. Palmer does not accept the existence of Lucifer or Satan, because he cannot conceive of a personal power of evil which is not the equal of God, as in the old Gnostic systems. Showing a complete lack of the New Testament and patristic scholarship, he argues that Gnosticism 'managed to capture certain intellectual heights within Christianity' and determined the development of Western academic theology.[100] That this view has been long untenable has been demonstrated by Bishop Stephen Neill's *The Interpretation of the New Testament, 1861–1961*.[101] To be fair to Palmer, he is less dogmatic in his *Living Christianity*.[102] Even a casual reading of the Bible would have shown him that there Satan does not have equal power with God but is a defeated foe: 'having spoiled principalities and powers, [Christ] made a shew of them openly, triumphing over them *in it*' (*Col. 2:15*), that is, in the cross.

We have already noted how Palmer rejects the biblical doctrine of election. But his criticism does not stop there. Concerning the forgiveness of sins he writes:

I find exclusive language, talk of Christ dying 'for all men' or praying that God will bestow peace 'on all men' equally offensive.[103]

He objects to such language, in part, because of what he regards as its 'sexist implications' (there is no recognition of woman kind), but he also insists that the idea of sin is to be rejected because it gives us a low expectation of ourselves.[104] The notions of sin and guilt are equally taboo in the New Age. Instead of thinking of sin, we should consider Christ, in whom 'we encounter the potential within us of all that God wishes to draw forth'.[105] Palmer is silent on the necessity of a transforming relationship with God. Instead, he describes him, in New Age language, as an exemplar of our human potential.

Palmer rejects Jesus' own explanations of the reason for his death.[106] He writes of both Anselm and Calvin as if they set up a concept of God from which they proceeded logically to deduce that reason, as if Jesus had not already advanced it. Anselm arbitrarily posited a God who was an immovable judge of justice.

Having set the conditions, God finds himself unable to forgive humanity, for to do so would be to deny his justice. Thus Jesus Christ came in order to take our sins upon himself and to be killed, in a sense by God, or at least for God, in order that the eternal nature of sin might be broken. Jesus took upon himself the death which was God's punishment for sin. Palmer comments, 'This, to my mind, horrific theology is called substitutionary atonement'.[107] But Anselm did not set up a God of any kind. He found in the Bible a God who was just, holy and loving, and a God who did not find a third party on whom to wreak vengeance, but a God who satisfied his love, justice and holiness by becoming man in order himself to do justice to his holiness and to express his heart of love for man by taking the just penalty for man's sin upon himself. Similarly, according to Palmer, Calvin started from the logical premise that man can be saved only by faith. But the doctrine of salvation by faith alone is no logical construction of Calvin. It is the plain and reiterated teaching of Scripture. From this premise, Palmer continues, Calvin reasoned that his concept of human nature demanded a God who could not act out of love or deviate from the strict rule of law.[108] The conclusion does not follow from the premise, but Palmer ignores the fallacy. He continues that since Calvin's arbitrarily created God could not deviate from law, he had from all eternity to predestinate some to eternal damnation and some to eternal life.[109] Again, there is no logical connection between premise and conclusion. Instead of trying to get into the mind of Anselm and Calvin, which he completely failed to do, a step necessitated by his hatred of their doctrine, he ought to have read his Bible, where he would have discovered that reconciling God's love and justice was God's problem, not Anselm's or Calvin's, a problem which he solved beautifully at Calvary, which is morally the most beautiful moment in the history of the universe. A New Ager to whom I explained the atonement simply, replied, 'If God did that, it was very beautiful.' Of Calvary, it can truly be said, 'Mercy and truth are met together; righteousness and peace have kissed each other' (*Ps. 85:10*).

It is because he rejected the idea of a substitutionary atonement that Palmer was able to take John Wesley's doctrine of holiness as an argument for the god within. Wesley's conversion on the 24 May, 1738, as he described it, resulted from the truth represented by the doctrine of the substitionary atonement: 'I felt my heart strangely warmed. I felt I did trust in Christ, Christ alone for salvation; and an assurance was given *me* that He had taken away *my* sins, even *mine*, and saved *me* from the law of sin and death.' In Wesley's teaching, justification brought about the new birth, which was the only entry into holiness:

While a man is in a mere natural state, before he is born of God, he has in a spiritual sense, eyes that see not; a thick impenetrable veil lies upon him. . . . Hence he has no knowledge of God, no intercourse with him; he is not at all acquainted with him.[110]

Holiness itself he defined as 'the life of God in the soul of man; a participation in the divine nature; the mind that was in Christ or, the renewal of our heart after the image of Him that created us'.[111] Whatever he taught about sinless perfection, he held that there was no holiness which was independent of the cross. The most sanctified Christian continued to need the merits of Christ.[112] It is therefore a travesty of Wesley's teaching to say that he regarded holiness as 'a long process of the realization of the divine within oneself'.[113] Palmer sees Wesley through New Age spectacles.

When we turn to what Palmer thinks about the cross, we find he cannot write about it without equating it with man's abuse of the environment. He cannot write of the two independently. Thus in *Living Christianity* he tells us:

The crucifixion is not just a historical event. It continues to happen every day of the year. Only now, we seem close to bringing much of God's creation, God's expression of love to an end – and a brutal and mocking end at that. It is when we see the crucifixion in these terms, as something which we are doing now, not something others did back in history, that we hear clearly what God wants to say to us through the death of Christ. . . . Can we hear the cry of Jesus, 'My God, my God, why have you forsaken me?' and be sure that such a cry is not going up from all creation?[114]

We found the same view in Matthew Fox, and promised to comment on the only possible Christian reaction to it. To equate the worst that man is doing to the earth with the death of Jesus, the Holy One of God, at the hands of sinful man is a scandal to the

Christian mind. It also shows that to the unregenerate mind the cross is the scandal of scandals. But the present danger to the ecosystem is of more concern to Palmer than Calvary. It is therefore no surprise to find him writing:

In the very varied bag of materials which are emerging from cross-cultural interaction and which are sometimes unhelpfully lumped together under the term 'New Age' we can see some remarkable new tellings of the stories of Christianity.[115]

This, as far as Martin Palmer and the New Age are concerned, says it all; the New Age is a valid and relevant statement of the Christian faith. How wrong-headed this view of the New Age is, we shall discover when we briefly review its tenets.

But since our study is about the relationship of the inter-faith movement and the New Age it is necessary to remind ourselves that at Assisi, Winchester and Coventry, Palmer showed himself to be an inter-faith activist. He is also an advocate of inter-faith in theory. He sees Christianity as only one of many stories of life on earth, which together form a series:

Within this, the Christian story is an integral part and has its role in helping bring to fruition or to grief certain other stories or sub-plots. But it is not the only story, and nor is it necessary for Christians to appear on each page, or even in each chapter.[116]

New stories of Christ arise in unexpected contexts, and from people and groups we did not intend to listen to, and confront us in places of which we had never dreamed:

In my own journey, the encounters have taken place . . . in Buddhist temples in Japan; at a gathering of the heads of environmental groups from around the world; . . . in Hindu temples in India and in Sikh gurdwaras in Manchester.[117]

He is not only a New Ager and an adherent of the inter-faith movement, he is also a syncretist. The only forms of Christianity of which he expresses approval are those which have been integrated with non-Christian elements, namely, Celtic Christianity and the Nestorian Chinese Christianity of the eighth century. In the former, shamanism and druidical elements were incorporated; in the latter, Christianity was imbued with Taoism.[118] It is all of a piece that he selects for special praise the address of Chung Hyan Kyung to the Canberra Assembly of the W.C.C. which was repudiated in its entirety by the Orthodox churches.[119]

As a protagonist of the god within and as a hankerer after monism Palmer cannot avoid the charge of being a New Ager; as an advocate of the inter-faith movement, he illustrates in his own person the connection between the New Age and the latter; as a syncretist he shows the direction to which the inter-faith movement and the New Age are both tending. His welcome by the institutional church bodes ill for its future.

The fight against oppression and injustice in all their forms and the struggle for peace which is part of the stated aims of both the advocates of inter-faith and the New Agers is something which Christians cannot object to and in which they must participate. God's opposition to man's inhumanity to man is voiced in Scripture no less than his insistence that he alone is to be worshipped, his jealousy for his glory on which the well-being of the whole creation depends. Christians may co-operate with men of good will everywhere in promoting these ends. This does not mean embracing the ideologies of non-Christians. Justice can be pursued without endorsing liberation theology, which involves the Marxist conception that man is in charge of his own history, in direct contradiction to the biblical view that God is sovereignly at work in history to bring it to a predetermined end. Equally, Christians must oppose the ideologies behind conservationism, which are pagan in origin.

That there is some danger of them doing so is evidenced by the Greenbelt Festival in August 1994. Greenbelt is an annual so-called evangelical event attended that year by 30,000 young people from Christian backgrounds. On this occasion its theme revolved around the images of creation, the tree of life and the rhythms of nature. It was inspired by the pagan *Gaia* hypothesis, not by the revelation of God's truth in his Word. But there is no reason for Christians to turn to paganism to show concern for the environment, for the Bible itself is a conservationist's handbook. As we pointed out earlier, the first man was appointed to 'till' the garden (*Gen. 2:15*), a verb used frequently in the Old Testament in the sense of 'worship'. Man was meant to tend the earth in a spirit of worship of its Creator, not of the creation, a role which precludes any ravaging or exploitation of it. The Bible contains the first prohibition in world literature of the policy of deforestation (*Deut. 20:19*). There are thus many causes in which believing man can co-operate with unbelieving man. This does not necessitate dialogue between religious groups on the presupposition that we are all seekers together. The Christian is possessed by Christ, who is the truth, the way and the life (*John 14:6*), and dialogue on the lines suggested by the W.C.C. would be a denial by the Christian of Christ's ownership of him. But joint action by believer and non-believer in humanitarian causes will give the Christian many opportunities for the dialogue envisaged in Scripture, the giving of a reason for the hope that is in him (*1 Pet. 3:15*). Humanitarian causes do not include one-world government. The only one-world government depicted in Scripture is the government to be assumed by the anti-Christ, if the book of Revelation is to be interpreted of future events, a view on which Christians may legitimately differ. But New Age literature as exemplified in Alice Bailey in any case reveals that the one-world government for which it is working would be totalitarian and inhumane in character.

The New Age movement represents in part a genuine search for truth on the part of men whom the churches have long abandoned to a spiritual vacuum. In the prevailing attitude of present-day Christendom towards biblical authority there is a famine of hearing the words of God (*Amos 8:11*). But in part the New Age movement also represents the normal tendency of unregenerate man to exalt himself against God and to worship the creation more than the Creator (*Rom. 1:18–20*), Who alone is blessed for ever (*Rom. 1:25*). It is man's yielding to the original lie, 'Ye shall be as gods' (*Gen. 3:5*). As such it is the continuation of mystery Babylon (*Rev. 17:8*), whose course and future are charted in the Bible: the religion of Babylon is the religion of the New Ager, to whom it could be equally said, 'Thy wisdom and thy knowledge, it hath perverted thee; and thou hast said in thine heart, I am and none else beside me' (*Isa. 47:10*), except, that is, the All that is also the I AM.

It is important to recognize that the mystical experience enjoyed by the New Ager after the transformation of his consciousness is identical with the mystical experience extolled by the inter-faith movement. In this experience, all dualities and separations, all objects and individuals, are seen as partial glimpses of the all-inclusive One, the ultimate Reality identified with pure consciousness, in the sense of unlimited and unconditional awareness. In Hindu terms, as Bede Griffiths has reminded us, it is *Saccidananda*, Being-Awareness-Bliss, the ecstasy of consciousness aware of itself. In the inter-faith movement, the symbols and rituals underlying each faith are welcomed as aids by which we encounter the depth of our being, for in the subjectivity and ego-centrism of the new spirituality we are told that to be in touch with God is to be in touch with ourselves. The mystics in the inter-faith movement declare with the New Agers, 'Man is God.' They too have succumbed to Satan's lie. Both the inter-faith movement and the New Age are expressions of the autonomous human consciousness in rebellion against God. Rejecting the God who has spoken, they take humanity as their starting point and therefore end with humanity as the ultimate. Beginning with the data of consciousness, they rearrange and reinterpret them. Following this procedure, it appears as self-evident that the fundamental principle of existence is consciousness itself. The image of God in which man was created, the heart of the self, is thus deified, and the creation exalted over the Creator. At the same time, the inter-faith movement and the New Age, by positing many Christs, deny the one Christ. For them Jesus Christ has not come in the flesh, and they are therefore expressions of the spirit of anti-Christ (*1 John 1:3*).

Some of the words of Karl Heim are apposite:

We cannot find God through a condition of ecstasy . . . As long as we are intoxicated we are not with God but only with ourselves. We are concerned with the swelling ocean of our own mental life. We can find God only in a spiritual act that occurs in deep solitude and with full mental clarity. That is why the Word plays the decisive role in the search for God.[120]

Christians ought to be more than chary when their activities meet with the unreserved approval of the devotees of Satan. Such an accolade has been granted to the inter-faith movement by the New Age organization World Goodwill, which in its newsletter for 1993, No. 4, has characterized 1993 as 'a year of interreligious understanding and co-operation'. It comments, 'A spiritual renaissance, the birthing of a global spirituality, is occurring in our time. This is taking place both outside the traditional preserves of religion and within them. The great varieties of religious initiatives for justice and peace is clear evidence of this. So, too, are the on-going dialogues between science, philosophy and the programmes of inter-faith co-operation celebrated in this newsletter.' It singles out for special praise the book of Hans Küng, *Global Responsibility: In Search of a New World Ethic* and the World Wildlife Fund's celebration at Assisi (1986), both of which we have studied. World Goodwill works under the aegis of the Lucis Trust, founded in 1922 as the Lucifer Publishing Company, adopting its present name in 1923, to disseminate the writings of Alice Bailey who ultimately succeeded Madame Blavatsky as leader of the Theosophical Society but left it when she began to receive transmissions from her own Ascended Masters. Her theme was the supersession of Christianity by a world religion. It was she who taught David Spangler that Lucifer was the 'bringer of light' or 'morning star' and denies that he is the Satan of 'conventional wisdom',[121] but 'morning star' is precisely the imagery in which the Bible describes Satan (*Isa. 14:12–14*). He is the ultimate author of Alice Bailey's Plan, which, in World Goodwill's current newsletter, using her own words, culiminates in a day 'when all religions will be regarded as emanating from one great spiritual source', which will come about when the churches fulfil their appointed task of enabling men to recognize 'the beauty of divinity in all forms', so that 'there will be neither Christian or heathen, neither Jew or Gentile, but simply one great body of believers, gathered out of all the current religions'. World Goodwill recognizes the inter-faith movement as a step in the fulfilment of this plan of its benevolent Lucifer (whom Christians know to be malignant), which indeed, if unconsciously, it is. *Caveat emptor* – in the vernacular, don't buy it.

World Goodwill not only approves of the inter-faith movement in the churches, but organizes its own inter-faith events. It has annually celebrated a World Invocation Day, described in its announcement of 13 June 1995 as the choice for that year, as a day when 'people of goodwill from all parts of the world, and from different political backgrounds' meet to invoke the 'advent of a Teacher, a spiritual leader or *Avatar*' who will 'inaugurate the coming of a new spiritual dimension', namely the fulfilment of Alice Bailey's Plan. It is proposed that in 1995 World Invocation Day shall be accompanied by 'The Christ's Festival', 'blending many different spiritual approaches in one united act of invocation'. We need here to remember the New Age definition of the Christ we noted earlier.[122] Further there is to be an Easter Festival and a Wesack Festival, the 'great eastern festival of the Buddha', expressing 'the keynotes of wisdom and divine purpose.'

EPILOGUE

The Claims and All-Sufficiency of Christ

The Claims and All-Sufficiency of Christ

The fact that we now live in a pluralist multi-faith society is no reason for playing down or abandoning the Great Commission of going into the world and making disciples of all nations as the adherents of the inter-faith movement would have us do, but a greater opportunity for proceeding with it. People of other faiths are now on our doorsteps. Evangelism need not and should not be carried out insensitively or aggressively, which the pluralists seem to consider it would inevitably involve. It must be accomplished by our lives more than our words; without a consistent life our words will be of no avail. If led by the Holy Spirit of God, a Christian will get alongside the other in loving concern before he will speak of his Lord, but speak he must. If Christ is the way, the truth and the life, without whom no-one can come to the Father, we have to make him known. If we do so abrasively, we may well turn away for life those whom we are seeking to win for him. But not to speak will also leave them without Christ and without hope in this life and the next.

'I am the way, the truth and the life: no man cometh to the Father but by me' is no isolated statement but the expression of a claim which runs through the whole of St. John's Gospel, which presents Christ from beginning to end as the only revealer of God: 'No man hath seen God at any time; the only begotten Son, which is in the bosom of the Father, he hath declared him' (*John 1:18*). Possessed of that intimate relationship with God, Christ heard his word and saw his deeds and repeated them: 'I do nothing of myself; but as my Father hath taught me, I speak these things' (*John 8:28*); 'The Son can do nothing of himself, but what he seeth the Father do: for whatsoever he doeth, these also doeth the Son likewise' (*John 5:19*). He was the perfect revealer of God because he was God. He did not come into being through his incarnation; before the incarnation he was already eternally God with God. Nor did he cease to be God when he became man: 'No man hath ascended up to heaven, but he that came down from heaven, even the Son of man which is in heaven' (*John 3:13*). He spoke more than once of his pre-incarnate existence: 'Before Abraham was, I am' (*John 8:58*), using the name by which God named himself in Exod. 3:13, 'I AM THAT I AM'. As God with God – in eternity, he possessed the glory of God: 'and now, O Father, glorify thou me with thine own self with the glory which I had with thee before the world was' (*John 17:5*). In all this we are on solid historical ground. New Testament scholarship is no longer unanimous that the Fourth Gospel contains meditations on the significance of Christ written long after his lifetime.

The Synoptic Gospels give us the same claims. It does not require a profound study of Jesus' encounter with the rich ruler described in Mark 10:18–27 to realize that to possess eternal life, to enter the kingdom of heaven, to follow Jesus and to be saved are synonymous phrases; to have eternal life, to belong to the kingdom of God and to be saved are dependent on following Jesus. We also have the explicit statment, 'No man knoweth the Son but the Father; neither knoweth any man the Father, save the Son, and he to whomsoever the Son will reveal him' (*Matt. 11:27*). The Son is the only way and the only revealer.

Sometimes it is argued on the basis of Philippians 2:6–7 ('Who being in the form of God, thought if not robbery to be equal with God: But made himself of no reputation, and took upon him the form of a servant, and was made in the likeness of men') that Christ in his earthly life divested himself of his divinity. But as B. B. Warfield as reminded us, everything that is said in the whole passage (*Phil. 2:5–11*) is undergirded by the assertion of his complete divinity; it is precisely because he was still in the form of God, that is, he 'still had in possession all that body of characterizing qualities by which God is made God . . . that he is said not to have been made not man, but in the likeness of men', to have been found not man, but 'in fashion as a man'.[1] By these phrases Paul is expressing his wonder at Christ's servanthood. It is the beauty and glory of Christ, the

Creator God (*John 1:3*) that he became man, without sin, to pay the price of our salvation.

We need not examine here the whole of the New Testament teaching about Christ's person, much less the foreshadowing of Christ in the Old Testament (even though the fact that before Christ there existed a body of literature about both his person and work, which cannot be said about the founder of any other religion, is an evidence of his uniqueness). It is sufficient to remind ourselves of his claims. We began this epilogue by enumerating them. In him we have a human teacher (though also divine) confronting religious people and telling him that he was the arbiter of their eternal destiny – 'I never knew you; depart from me ye that work iniquity'. To those broken down by life he said, 'Come unto me all ye that labour and are heavy laden, and I will give you rest'. He claimed a kingship greater than that of David and Solomon – 'David therefore called him Lord'; 'Behold, a greater than Solomon is here'. He declared himself to have a heavenly origin, 'Ye are from beneath, I am from above'. He spoke of his power to bestow eternal life: 'He that heareth my word, and believeth on him that sent me, hath everlasting life, and shall not come into condemnation, but is passed from death unto life'. He challenged his hearers to find any sin in him, 'Which of you convinceth me of sin?'

If these words are not true, Jesus was self-deceived or set out to deceive, possibilities ruled out by the life he lived. There is no escaping Augustine's alternative, 'Either God or not good'. Christ was indeed 'holy, harmless, undefiled, separate from sinners' (*Heb. 7:26*). We use 'harmless' in a perjorative sense of someone who made no great mark for good or evil. A truly harmless man, however, is a miracle. Which of us, whatever faith, has not done or received harm? But Jesus spent his earthly life 'doing good, and healing all that were oppressed by the devil' (*Acts 21:38*).

If any other man laid claim to moral perfection his faults and delinquencies would rapidly lay him open to ridicule and contempt. But although he required repentance from all others as a necessity of entering the kingdom of God, Jesus lived with no confession of repentance on his own part, no fear or look of contrition and no request to heaven for pardon. He began with an impenitent or unrepentant piety and held it the end, without bringing any visible stain upon it. No charge was ever brought against his character. It was his claims which his antagonists brought against him. They were blind to his authentication of his claims by his life even though they possessed in the Old Testament evidence which ought to have led them to accept him: 'Search the Scriptures for . . . they are they which testify of me' (*John 5:39*).

Much academic New Testament scholarship has argued that the Gospels record the impression Jesus made on the early church, rather than a depiction of Jesus as he was in himself. This creates the insuperable problem of how their authors were able to portray a character of moral perfection which lay completely outside their experience until Jesus himself appeared. Writers can only write from their own observation of life. For the Gospel writers to have written as they did, they must have encountered in Jesus an example of flawless perfection.

So we return to his irrefutable claims. 'I am the light of the world: he that followeth me shall not walk in darkness, but shall have the light of life' (*John 8:12*). Since with him light came into the world, why should we follow the supporters of the inter-faith movement and seek light elsewhere? The light of Christ cannot be enhanced. The inter-faith movement seeks to add to it by searching for further light where there are only glimmerings shrouded by darkness. There are glimmerings of light in other faiths because they reflect the obscured image of God in fallen man, but they are glimmering in the darkness which they cannot dissipate, because 'the God of this world hath blinded the minds of them which believe not, lest the light of the glorious gospel of Christ, who is the image of God, should shine into them' (*2 Cor. 4:4*). In no-one else shall we find the very brightness of the glory of God (*Heb. 1:3*). From none other shall we hear words which are spirit and life (*John 6:63*). To whom else can we go? To whom else can we point the nations, from all of which he is calling out his church?

NOTES

1 *The Inter-Faith Movement: A Preliminary Survey*

1. *World Faiths Insight*, the joint magazine of the London-based World Congress of Faiths and the New York-based Temple of Understanding, Washington, D.C., (Spring 1977).
2. *Vital Religion*, cited by George Seaver, *Francis Younghusband, Explorer and Mystic* (London: Murray, 1952), p. 249. Seaver's biography is hereafter referred to as *Younghusband*.
3. *Younghusband*, p. 98.
4. Ibid.
5. Ibid., p. 99.
6. *World Faiths*, No. 99 (Summer 1976), p. 4.
7. *Modern Mystics*, Younghusband (London: Murray, 1935), pp. 214–30.
8. Ibid., p. 243.
9. Ibid., p. 246.
10. Ibid., Preface, p. vii.
11. Quoted by Seaver, *Younghusband*, p. 164.
12. Ibid.
13. *World Faiths*, No. 66 (Summer 1966), p. 14.
14. *World Faiths*, No. 91 (1973), p. 3.
15. *World Faiths*, No. 94 (1974), p. 5.
16. Ibid., p. 2.
17. *The Temple of Understanding News Letter*, Washington, D.C., (Spring 1976).
18. *World Faiths*, No. 81, (1970), p. 3.
19. *No Other Name: The Choice between Syncretism and Christian Universalism*, Visser't Hooft (London: S.C.M., 1963), p. 11.
20. *Christian Herald*, 24 March, 1990.
21. *Christian Herald*, 20 March, 1993.
22. Quoted by Alan Morrison, *The Serpent and the Cross* (Birmingham: K. & M. Books), p. 554.
23. *Sunrise*, the official journal of the Theosophical Society, Vol. 42, No. 1, 1992.
24. K. E. Tolbert, *Christian News* (Trenton, Missouri, 20 September 1993), p. 15, quoted by Morrison, *The Serpent and the Cross*, pp. 555–6.
25. *Mission, Dialogue and Inter-Religious Encounter*, (London: Inter-Faith Network, 1993), p. 6.

11 *Pluralists and Syncretists: The Theologians and Inter-Faith*

1. *The Myth of Christian Uniqueness*, eds., John Hick and Paul F. Knitter (London: S.C.M., 1988), p. viii.
2. Ibid., p. 162.
3. Ibid., p. 8ff.
4. Ibid., p. 23.
5. Ibid., p. 23.
6. Ibid., p. 12.
7. Ibid., p. 37.
8. Ibid., p. 59.
9. Ibid., p. 69.
10. Ibid., p. 32.
11. Ibid., pp. 117–34.
12. Ibid., p. 122.
13. Ibid., p. 125.
14. Ibid., p. 126.
15. Ibid., p. 127.
16. Ibid., p. 128.
17. Ibid., p. 130.
18. Ibid., p. 129.
19. Ibid., p. 130.
20. Ibid., pp. 89–116.
21. Ibid., p. 112.
22. Ibid., p. 114.
23. Ibid., p. 108.
24. Ibid., pp. 32–3.
25. Ibid., p. 33.
26. See *The Gospel according to St. Mark*, Cambridge Greek Testament Commentary, C. E. B. Cranfield (C.U.P.: 1966), pp. 343–4.
27. *Myth of Christian Uniqueness*, p. 78.
28. Ibid., p. 39.
29. Ibid., pp. 49–50.
30. Ibid., pp. 53–5.
31. Ibid., p. 141.
32. Ibid., p. 77.
33. Ibid., p. 79.
34. Ibid., p. 79.
35. Ibid., p. 41.
36. Ibid., p. 41.
37. Ibid., p. 43.
38. Ibid., p. 43.
39. Ibid., pp. 137–200.
40. Ibid., p. 174.
41. Ibid., p. 185.

42. Ibid., p. 191.

43. Ibid., p. 192.

44. Ibid., pp. 193–4.

45. Ibid., p. 195.

46. Ibid., p. 180.

47. Ibid., p. 189.

48. Ibid., p. 102.

49. *Global Responsibility: In Search of a World Ethic*, Hans Küng (London: S.C.M., 1991), p. xv.

50. Ibid., p. 138.

51. *World Faiths*, No. 84, (1971), pp. 5–6.

52. *Global Responsibility*, p. 102.

53. Quoted by K. Spink, *A Sense of the Sacred, A Biography of Bede Griffiths* (London: S.P.C.K., 1988), p. 32.

54. *Christian Ashram*, A. R. Griffiths (London: Darton, Longman and Todd, 1966), p. 25.

55. Ibid., p. 171.

56. Ibid., p. 20.

57. *Return to the Centre*, A. R. Griffiths (London: Collins, 1976), p. 15.

58. Ibid., p. 107.

59. *Christian Ashram*, p. 36.

60. *Return to the Centre*, p. 68.

61. Ibid., pp. 86–7.

62. *Christian Ashram*, p. 177.

63. Ibid., p. 30.

64. *Return to the Centre*, p. 106.

65. Ibid., p. 101.

66. Ibid., p. 100.

67. *Christian Ashram*, pp. 89–90.

68. Ibid., p. 74.

69. *Return to the Centre*, p. 63.

70. *Letters and Papers from Prison*, Dietrich Bonhoeffer (London: Fontana, 1964), p. 56.

71. *Return to the Centre*, p. 89.

72. *Asian Journal of Thomas Merton*, Thomas Merton (London: Sheldon Press, 1974), p. 17.

73. Ibid., p. 115.

74. Ibid., p. 276.

75. Ibid., p. 277.

76. *Zen and the Birds of Appetite*, Thomas Merton (New Directions Publishing, 1968), p. 86.

77. Ibid., p. 134.

78. *Mystics and Zen Masters*, Thomas Merton (New York: Dell, 1978), p. 228.

79. *Asian Journal*, pp. 114–5.

80. Marco Pallis, cited in the *Asian Journal*, pp. 114–5.

81. *Asian Journal*, p. 332.

82. *Zen and the Birds of Appetite*, p. 45.
83. *Asian Journal*, p. 340.
84. *Thomas Merton and Asia: His Quest for Utopia*, A. Lipski, (Kalamazoo, Michigan: Cistercian Publications, 1982), p. 5.
85. *Zen and the Birds of Appetite*, p. 9.
86. Ibid., p. 11.
87. Ibid., p. 5.
88. Ibid., p. 5.
89. *Asian Journal*, pp. 82–8, 271.
90. Ibid., p. 64.
91. Ibid., p. 323.
92. Ibid., p. 143.
93. Ibid., pp. 233–6.
94. *The Cross of Christ* (Leicester: I.V.P., 1986), pp. 335–6.
95. *Opening the Bible*, Thomas Merton (London: Allen and Unwin, 1972), p. 51.
96. Lipski, *Thomas Merton in Asia*, p. 50.
97. *Asian Journal*, p. 353.
98. Ibid., p. 343.
99. Ibid., p. 308.
100. *Orthodoxy and the Religion of the Future* (Platina, California: Saint Herman of Alaska Brotherhood, 1975), quoted by J. Cotter, *A Study in Syncretism* (Ontario, 1983), p. 72.
101. *The Golden Book of the Theosophical Society*, 1925, pp. 28–29, cited by Constance Cumbrey, *The Hidden Dangers of the Rainbow* (Shreveport, Louisiana: Huntington House Inc., 1983), p. 44.
102. Cited by D. R. Groothius in *Unmasking the New Age* (Illinois: I.V.P., 1986), p. 181.
103. Cited by Constance Cumbrey, *The Hidden Dangers of the Rainbow*, p. 45.
104. Ibid., p. 45.

III *The Churches and Inter-Faith*

1. *The Documents of Vatican II* (London: Chapman, 1967), p. 35; cf. *Other Faiths: What Does the Church Teach?* (London: Catholic Truth Society, 1986), pp. 20–1.
2. *Commentary on St John's Gospel*, C. K. Barrett (London: S.P.C.K., 1955), p. 134.
3. Ibid., pp. 127–9.
4. Ibid., p. 134.
5. *Documents of Vatican II*, p. 662. Emphasis added.
6. *Documents of Vatican II*, pp. 661–3.
7. *Other Faiths*, pp. 18–19.
8. *L'Osservatore Romano*, 10 February, 1986.

9. Ibid., 14 March, 1986.
10. Ibid., 6 September, 1986.
11. *L'Osservatore Romano*, 27 October, 1986.
12. *L'Osservatore Romano*, 27 October, 1986.
13. *L'Osservatore Romano*, 2 November, 1986.
14. *L'Osservatore Romano*, 13 October, 1986.
15. *Prophetic Alert*, Secunderabad, March, 1986.
16. *Other Faiths*, p. 19.
17. Ibid., p. 12.
18. *Catholic World*, May–June 1989, p. 125.
19. Ibid., p. 100.
20. Ibid., pp. 100–101.
21. *Origins, CNS documentary service*, 19 March, 1992, Vol. 21, No. 41, USA.
22. *The Trumpet* (S. Aurora, Colorado: National Research Institute, November/December 1990).
23. I discuss this further below, p. 111.
24. *World Faiths*, No. 103 (1977), p. 3.
25. 'The Authority of the Bible' in *The Ecumenical Review* (Geneva, October 1971), pp. 426–35.
26. *Breaking Barriers, Nairobi 1975*, ed., D. M. Paton (London: S.P.C.K., 1976), p. 254.
27. *Uppsala to Nairobi, 1968–1975*, ed., D. E. Johnson (London: S.P.C.K., 1975), pp. 14–5.
28. *World Faiths*, No. 83 (1971), pp. 23–4.
29. *Faith in the Midst of Faiths: Reflections on Dialogue in Community*, ed. S. J. Samartha (Geneva: W.C.C., 1977), pp. 18–25.
30. Ibid., p. 30.
31. Ibid., p. 33.
32. Ibid., p. 75.
33. Ibid., p. 143.
34. Ibid., p. 145.
35. *Uppsala to Nairobi, 1968–1975*, p. 106.
36. *Breaking Barriers*, p. 76.
37. *Faith in the Midst of Faiths*, p. 99.
38. Ibid., p. 75.
39. *Uppsala to Nairobi*, p. 106.
40. *Breaking Barriers*, p. 76.
41. *World Faiths*, No. 100 (1976), pp. 34–5.
42. *Breaking Barriers*, p. 72.
43. *World Faiths*, No. 100 (1976), p. 38.
44. *Uppsala to Nairobi*, p. 98.
45. *Breaking Barriers*, p. 74.
46. *Faith in the Midst of Faiths*, p. 91.
47. Ibid.
48. Ibid., p. 92.
49. Ibid., p. 33.

50. *Uppsala to Nairobi*, p. 107.
51. *Faith in the Midst of Faiths*, p. 129.
52. Ibid., p. 145.
53. *Breaking Barriers*, p. 83.
54. See above, p. 40.
55. *Contextualization: A Theology of Gospel and Culture*, Bruce Nicholls (Exeter: Paternoster Press, 1979), p. 62.
56. *What About Other Faiths?*, M. Goldsmith (London: Hodder and Stoughton, 1989), pp. 147–8.
57. *Gathered for Life*, Official Report VI Assembly, ed., D. Gill (Geneva: W.C.C., 1983), p. 31.
58. *Vancouver to Canberra, 1983–1990*, ed., T. E. Best (Geneva: W.C.C., 1991), p. 137.
59. Ibid., p. 135.
60. See above, pp. 38–9.
61. *Spirituality in Inter-Faith Dialogue*, ed., Tosh Arai and Wesley Ariarajah (Geneva: W.C.C., 1989), p. 8.
62. Ibid., p. 18.
63. Ibid., p. 35.
64. Ibid., p. 39.
65. Ibid., p. 50.
66. Ibid., pp. 47–8.
67. Ibid., p. 53.
68. Ibid., p. 100.
69. *Gathered for Life*, p. 15.
70. Ibid., p. 255.
71. *International Review of Mission*, Geneva, April 1990, p. 192.
72. On World Goodwill see below pp. 184–5.
73. *Signs of the Spirit*, Official Report of the Seventh Assembly, ed. M. Kinnamon (Geneva: W.C.C., 1991), p. 13.
74. Ibid., p. 13.
75. Ibid., pp. 38–9.
76. Ibid., p. 39.
77. *The Australian*, 11 February, 1991.
78. *The Bible and People of Other Faiths* (Geneva: W.C.C., 1985), p. 65.
79. *Who was Jesus?*, N. T. Wright (London: S.P.C.K., 1992), p. 103.
80. *Signs of the Spirit*, pp. 280–1.
81. *Canberra Take-Aways* (Geneva: W.C.C., 1991), p. 26.
82. *The Australian Beacon*, No. 338, August, 1994. On the alleged feminine origin of the divine wisdom, see below pp. 136–7.
83. *Christian Herald*, 30 June 1990.
84. Ibid.
85. *Multi-Faith Worship?*, p. 18.
86. See above, pp. 69–70.
87. *Towards a New Relationship*, K. Cracknell (London: Epworth Press, 1986), p. 102.
88. *Multi-Faith Worship?*, p. 20.

89. Ibid.
90. Ibid., p. 21.
91. Ibid., p. 26.
92. *Haggai, Zechaiah, Malachi*, Tyndale O.T. Commentaries (Leicester: I.V.P., 1972), pp. 228–30.
93. *Multi-Faith Worship?*, p. 22.
94. Ibid., p. 50.
95. Ibid., p. 54.
96. Ibid., p. 55.

IV *Environmentalism and Inter-Faith*

1. *Religion and Nature Inter-Faith Ceremony*, W.W.F. 25th Anniversary, 29 September, 1986, p. 12.
2. Ibid., p. 18.
3. Ibid., p. 20.
4. Ibid., p. 26.
5. Ibid., p. 27.
6. Ibid., p. 30.
7. Ibid., p. 43.
8. *The Assisi Declarations* (W.W.F., 1986), p. 6.
9. Ibid., p. 17.
10. Ibid.
11. Ibid., p. 18.
12. Ibid., p. 19.
13. *Faith and Nature*, ed., Martin Palmer, (W.W.F. Century Paperback, Hutchison), p. 53.
14. *Creation and Harvest Service Book*, (W.W.F., Godalming), p. 35.
15. *Genesis or Nemesis, belief, meaning and ecology*, (Dryad Press, 1988), pp. 30–31.
16. Ibid., p. 31.
17. *Colossians & Philemon Studies* (London: Pickering & Inglis, n.d.), pp. 88–89.
18. *Creation and Harvest Service Book*, p. 44.
19. *A Basket of Fragments*, R. M. McCheyne (Inverness: Christian Focus Publications, 1975), p. 172.
20. *Creation and Harvest Service Book*, p. 46.
21. Ibid., pp. 5–6, 9, 31, 33–4, 47.
22. Ibid., p. 4.
23. Ibid., p. 33.
24. Ibid., p. 34.
25. *Genesis or Nemesis*, p. 112.
26. cf. *Creation and Harvest Service Book*, pp. 8–9.
27. *Assisi Declarations*, pp. 18–9.
28. *Human Energy*, Teilhard de Chardin (London: Collins, 1969), pp. 107–8.

29. Ibid., pp. 57–8.
30. Ibid., p. 47.
31. Ibid., p. 46.
32. Ibid., p. 70.
33. Ibid.
34. Ibid., pp. 70–71.
35. Ibid., p. 97.
36. Ibid., p. 96.
37. Ibid., p. 95.
38. Ibic., l.c.
39. Ibid., p. 96.
40. Ibid.
41. *The Phenomenon of Man*, Teilhard de Chardin (London: Fontana Books, Collins), p. 62.
42. *Human Energy*, p. 100.
43. Ibid., p. 158.
44. Ibid., p. 91.
45. Ibid., pp. 83–4.
46. Ibid., p. 91.
47. Ibid., footnote, p. 69.
48. *The Phenomenon of Man*, pp. 70–2, 298–9.
49. *Human Energy*, pp. 32, 41.
50. Ibid., p. 62.
51. Ibid., p. 32.
52. Ibid., p. 31.
53. Ibid.
54. Ibid., p. 35.
55. Ibid.
56. Ibid., pp. 37–8.
57. Ibid., p. 42.
58. Ibid., p. 47.
59. Ibid.
60. Ibid., pp. 106–7.
61. *The Phenomenon of Man*, p. 75.
62. *Human Energy*, p. 29.
63. *Letters to Two Friends, 1926–1952* (New York: Meridian Books, 1969), p. 154.
64. *Human Energy*, p. 91.
65. Ibid.
66. Ibid., p. 92.
67. *The Phenomenon of Man*, p. 322.
68. Ibid., p. 321.
69. *Human Energy*, p. 139.
70. Ibid., p. 51.
71. Ibid., p. 52.
72. Ibid.
73. Ibid., p. 91.

74. Ibid., p. 156.
75. E.g., *The Coming of the Cosmic Christ*, Matthew Fox (San Francisco: Harper, 1988), pp. 6, 92.
76. *Original Blessing*, Matthew Fox (Santa Fe: Bear & Co., 1983), p. 71.
77. *The Coming of the Cosmic Christ*, p. 176.
78. Ibid., pp. 225–7.
79. *Original Blessing*, p. 16.
80. *A Planned Deception, the Staging of a New Age Messiah*, Constance Cumbrey (Michigan: Pointe Publishers, 1985), p. 139.
81. *Original Blessing*, ibid.
82. *Whee! We, Wee, All The Way Home, A Guide to Sensual Prophetic Spirituality*, M. Fox (Santa Fe: Bear & Co., 1981), pp. 30, 240.
83. *Original Blessing*, p. 89.
84. Ibid.
85. Ibid., p. 210.
86. *The Coming of the Cosmic Christ*, p. 57.
87. *Original Blessing*, p. 224.
88. Ibid., p. 28.
89. Ibid., p. 40.
90. *Creation Spirituality, Liberating Gifts for the Peoples of the Earth*, M. Fox (San Francisco: Harper, 1991), p. 5.
91. *Original Blessing*, p. 123.
92. Ibid., p. 255.
93. *A Spirituality Named Compassion and the Healing of the Global Village, Humpty Dumpty and Us*, M. Fox (Minneapolis: Winston Press, 1974), p. 34.
94. *The Coming of the Cosmic Christ*, p. 153.
95. Ibid., p. 94.
96. Ibid., p. 183.
97. Ibid., p. 43.
98. *Myth of Christian Uniqueness*, pp. 144–8.
99. *The Coming of the Cosmic Christ*, p. 11.
100. Ibid., p. 240.
101. Ibid., p. 243.
102. Ibid., p. 231.
103. Ibid.
104. *Original Blessing*, p. 166; cf. p. 239.
105. Ibid., p. 164.
106. Ibid., p. 266.
107. Ibid., p. 243.
108. Ibid.
109. Ibid., p. 171; *The Coming of the Cosmic Christ*, p. 71.
110. *The Coming of the Cosmic Christ*, p. 140.
111. Ibid., p. 147.
112. Ibid., p. 149.
113. *Original Blessing*, pp. 48, 85, 111.
114. Ibid., pp. 19, 44.

115. Ibid., p. 47.
116. Ibid., pp. 18–9.
117. Ibid., pp. 19, 46, 105.
118. Ibid., p. 49.
119. Ibid., p. 51.
120. Ibid., p. 54.
121. Ibid., pp. 265–83 passim.
122. Ibid., p. 82.
123. Ibid., p. 110.
124. Ibid., p. 111.
125. Ibid., pp. 19–20.
126. Ibid., p. 162.
127. Ibid., p. 296.
128. Ibid., p. 24.
129. Ibid., p. 15.
130. *Creation Spirituality*, p. 18.
131. Ibid., p. 8.
132. Ibid.
133. Ibid., p. 10.
134. *Original Blessing*, p. 59.
135. Ibid., p. 63.
136. *The Coming of the Cosmic Christ*, pp. 146–7.
137. *Original Blessing*, p. 69.
138. Ibid.
139. Ibid., p. 138.
140. *The Coming of the Cosmic Christ*, p. 239.
141. Ibid.
142. *Original Blessing*, pp. 50, 24.
143. Ibid., p. 23.
144. Ibid., p. 24.
145. *Creation Spirituality*, p. 21.
146. *Original Blessing*, p. 180.
147. Ibid., p. 181.
148. Ibid., p. 183.
149. Ibid., p. 184.
150. Ibid., p. 187.
151. Ibid., pp. 191–4.
152. Ibid., pp. 202–3.
153. Ibid., pp. 203–4.
154. Ibid., p. 204.
155. Ibid., p. 205.
156. Ibid., p. 218.
157. Ibid., p. 219.
158. Ibid.
159. Ibid., p. 251.
160. Ibid.
161. Ibid., pp. 225–6.

162. Ibid., p. 260.
163. Ibid., p. 261.
164. Ibid., pp. 262–3.
165. Ibid., p. 264.
166. Ibid.
167. Ibid., p. 270.
168. Ibid., pp. 281–2.
169. *The Coming of the Cosmic Christ*, p. 2.
170. Ibid., p. 176.
171. Ibid., p. 164.
172. Ibid., p. 177.
173. Ibid.
174. *The Aquarian Conspiracy*, Marilyn Ferguson (London: Paladin Books, 1984), pp. 168–9, 234.

v *Inter-Faith and the New Age*

1. *God, Revelation and Authority*, Vol. 1, (Waco, Texas), p. 70.
2. *Out on a Limb* (New York: Bantam), p. 236.
3. *Reflections on the Christ* (Findhorn Publications, 1978), p. 14.
4. Ibid., p. 16.
5. Ibid., p. 28.
6. *Towards a Planetary Vision* (Findhorn Publications, 1977), p. 30.
7. Ibid., p. 12; see above, p. 32.
8. *Conversations with John* (Lorian Press), p. 32; cf. *Reflections on the Christ*, p. 101.
9. *Reflections on the Christ*, p. 107.
10. *Conversations with John*, p. 22.
11. *Reflections on the Christ*, p. 129.
12. Ibid., pp. 14–5.
13. *Towards a Planetary Vision*, p. 40.
14. *A Course in Miracles* (Foundation for Inner Peace, 1975), Vol. 1, pp. 32–3.
15. *Reflections on the Christ*, p. 7.
16. Ibid., p. 61.
17. *The Laws of Manifestation* (Findhorn Publications, 1981), p. 72.
18. Ibid., p. 73.
19. *The Counterfeit Christ*, Ron Rhodes (Grand Rapids: Baker Book House, 1991.
20. Quoted by W. Martin *The New Age Cult* (Minneapolis: Bethany House Publishers, 1989), p. 18.
21. See above, p. 46.
22. *Theosophy: Key to Understanding* (Wheaton: Theosophical Publishing House, 1967), p. 122.
23. *The Aquarian Conspiracy*, Marilyn Ferguson, p. 93.

24. Foreword to Surjit Singh's *Christology and Personality* (Philadelphia: Westminster Press, 1961), p. 14.
25. *Gaia, the practical science of planetary medicine* (London & Stroud: Gaia Books, 1991), p. 17.
26. *Well Body, Well Earth* (San Francisco: Sierra Club Books, 1983), p. 69.
27. *Unmasking the New Age. Is There A New Religious Movement Trying to Transform Society?* (Illinois: I.V.P., 1986), pp. 133–4.
28. *The Book of the Goddess Past and Present* (New York: The Crossroad Publishing Company, 1989), p. 49.
29. Ynestra King, in *Healing the Wounds* (Santa Cruz: New Society Publishers, 1989), p. 19.
30. See above, p. 132.
31. *The Spiral Dance* (Harper and Row, 1979), p. 25.
32. Ibid., p. 9.
33. Ibid., p. 129.
34. Barbara Walker, *The Woman's Encyclopedia of Myths and Secrets* (San Francisco: Harper and Row, 1983), p. 346.
35. *Unmasking the New Age*, p. 138.
36. *God, Revelation and Authority*, Waco, Texas, vol. 5, p. 159.
37. *Women and the Word of God: A Response to Biblical Feminism* (Grand Rapids: Baker, 1980), p. 153.
38. Rosemary Ruether, 'Goddesses and Witches' in *The Christian Century*, September, 1990, p. 843.
39. *The Dream of the Earth* (San Francisco: Sierra Club Books, 1988), p. 48.
40. *Wilderness, The Way Ahead*, eds. Vance Martin and Mary Inglis (Findhorn Press, Lorian Press, 1984), p. 314.
41. *Wilderness*, ed. Vance Martin (The Findhorn Press, 1982), p. 71.
42. Ibid., p. 70.
43. Ibid., p. 68.
44. *Wilderness, The Way Ahead*, p. 232.
45. *For the Conservation of the Earth*, ed. Vance Martin (Colorado: Fulcrum Golden, 1987), p. 307.
46. *Reflections on the Christ*, p. 39.
47. See above, pp. 94–7.
48. See above, p. 116.
49. See above, p. 110.
50. *The Turning Point* (London: Flamingo, 1983), pp. 69–70.
51. *The Tao of Physics* (Harper Collins, Wildwood House, 1991), p. 11.
52. Ibid., p. 151.
53. *The Turning Point*, p. 410.
54. See above, p. 46.
55. *The Turning Point*, p. 80.
56. *New Genesis, Shaping a Global Spirituality*, Robert Muller (New York: Image Books, Doubleday & Co., Inc., 1984).

57. Ibid., p. 160.
58. Ibid., p. 161.
59. Ibid., p. 162.
60. Ibid., p. 163.
61. Ibid., p. 164.
62. Ibid.
63. Ibid., p. 167.
64. Ibid., p. 166. Emphasis added.
65. Ibid., p. 171.
66. Ibid.
67. Ibid., p. 178.
68. Quoted by Martin, op. cit., pp. 65–6.
69. *Earth at Omega: Passage to Planetization* (Boston: Branden Press, 1982), p. iii.
70. *The Initiator*, September 1983. Emphasis added.
71. Quoted by Martin, op. cit., p. 65.
72. *Circle Network News*, Fall 1983, quoted by C. E. Cumbrey, *A Planned Deception, The Staging of a New Age Messiah*, p. 138. Emphasis added.
73. *The Christian Herald*, 25 June 1994.
74. *Living Christianity*, Martin Palmer (Dorset: Element, 1993), p. 165. Emphasis added.
75. Ibid., p. 15.
76. Ibid.
77. *Coming of Age, An Exploration of Christianity and the New Age*, Martin Palmer (London: Aquarian/Thorson, 1993), p. 47.
78. Ibid., p. 48.
79. p. 9. Palmer wishes me to give more of the context of this passage. Here he explains that these activities did not represent a spiritual search, but an interest in out of the way ideas, and a sympathy for those who held them because of the general contempt which they thus earned. This does not alter the fact that his activities brought him into divinely forbidden territory which could only have had a spiritually harmful effect on him.
80. Ibid., p. 12.
81. See above, p. 42.
82. See above, p. 145.
83. *Coming of Age*, pp. 93–5.
84. Ibid., p. 94.
85. Ibid., pp. 97–8.
86. Ibid., p. 97.
87. Ibid., p. 180.
88. Ibid., p. 181. Palmer wishes me to say that here he was merely trying to point out that a purely rational approach to God was inadequate. But there is no escaping his definite statement that God spoke to him through the I Ching.
89. Ibid.

90. Ibid., p. 182.
91. Ibid., p. 151.
92. See above, pp. 122, 125.
93. See above, pp. 150–1.
94. *Coming of Age*, p. 150.
95. See above, p. 127.
96. Ibid., p. 23. Here Palmer asks me to point out he was quoting another author, a feminist, and was not necessarily agreeing with her.
97. Ibid., p. 164.
98. *Reflections on the Christ*, pp. 36–9.
99. *Exploration: Emerging Aspects of the New Planetary Culture* (Findhorn, 1980), p. 106.
100. *Coming of Age*, p. 89.
101. *The Interpretation of the New Testament, 1861–1961*, Stephen Neill (Oxford paperbacks, 1966), esp. pp. 180–1 and footnotes.
102. *Living Christianity*, p. 25.
103. Ibid., p. 139.
104. Ibid., p. 174.
105. Ibid., p. 177.
106. See above, pp. 31–2.
107. *Living Christianity*, p. 46.
108. Ibid., p. 60.
109. Ibid.
110. Quoted by A. Skevington Wood, *The Burning Heart* (Bethany House Publishers, 1978), p. 246.
111. Ibid., p. 267.
112. Ibid., p. 268.
113. *Coming of Age*, p. 47.
114. Ibid., p. 191. Palmer makes the same identification in a letter to me but contends 'Far from ignoring the cross, I take it so seriously that it shapes my understanding of all life'. He thus takes the subjective view of the atonement: its importance is its effect on us. But that is not its prime importance. The atonement was an act of God intended to have the objective result of conferring on those who respond to it a new legal standing before God, that of an adoptive sonship. This is the necessary preliminary to the reshaping of our attitudes, itself the work of the Holy Spirit. Palmer's rejection of the objective nature of the atonement follows from his rejections of penal substitution. The cross which is significant to him is not the biblical cross.
115. Ibid., p. 187.
116. Ibid., p. 185.
117. Ibid., p. 188.
118. Ibid., pp. 67–70, 109–14.
119. Ibid., pp. 143–45; see Ch. III, pp. 000–00.
120. *The Spirit of Protestantism* (Philadelphia: Fortress Press, 1963), p. 247.
121. Constance Cumbrey, *A Planned Deception*, p. 246.
122. See above, pp. 154–5.

Epilogue

1. *The Person and Work of Christ* (Philadelphia: The Presbyterian and Reformed Publishing House, 1950), p. 41.

Index

Index

Index

Index

Index

Index